Without
Firing a
Shot

Without Firing a Shot

The Death of American Liberty through Political Correctness

Ron Walker

To order additional copies of this book, contact:
Roncore Media
www.roncoremedia.com
Or order directly from:
www.withoutfiringashot.com

CONTENTS

This book is dedicated to the following people
for reasons I will explain later:

Charles R. Walker Sr.
Blanche Alice Walker
Susannah A. Walker
Jessica Walker Catchpole
Elaine Jeffs

Knowledge will forever govern ignorance; and a people who mean to be their own governors must arm themselves with the power which knowledge gives.

—James Madison

INTRODUCTION

Patriotism is supporting your country all the time, and your government when it deserves it.

—Mark Twain

T he American Revolution was primarily fought by average citizens who came to realize that too many aspects of their everyday lives were being controlled by a tyrannical British government. For most of my life, I have noticed a slow and methodical effort on the part of some to create that same tyranny in today's American government through subliminal mind control of the people. Once again, the time has come for the average citizen in this country to answer a call to arms. Not with musket rifles but with something far less bloody and much more powerful: the truth.

As a child growing up in the 1960s, I heard the popular catchphrases and saw the symbolism of the day—of which there was plenty. I saw people use the two-fingered V-shaped sign for peace, or wear a peace symbol around their necks. Occasionally, I would see the peace symbol worn as a patch on an old army shirt. I must admit, I was far too young and naive at the time to pick up on the irony of a peace symbol worn on military clothing—I thought it just looked cool.

Hardly a day would go by without seeing students and other young people on the evening news protesting about the Vietnam War and holding up homemade signs, which read, "Make love, not war!" Some of those protests became violent as the protesters would speak of starting one revolution or another to end the war and change the government of the United States. The irony and hypocrisy of people protesting a war by promoting a violent revolution in order to bring about peace did not escape me.

As I reached my late teens and early twenties, I began to better understand what the protests were all about—if only in principle. I began to recognize the injustices around me and felt a deep need to become part of the inevitable generational desire to right the wrongs and create a better world. In spite of these feelings, however, I found myself hesitant to join the fight. Something didn't feel right about the messages I was hearing. I felt I wasn't being given the whole story—or at least that I was getting a distorted version of the stories, so I did nothing.

I asked myself, "If this were true, for what purpose was I and the rest of the world being misled? And to what end? Why would anyone speak of fighting for such worthy causes as world peace or an end to poverty and hunger if these were not their true goals? If the changes they wanted to see were truly needed, and the method required to bring about those changes was necessary and just, why would they need to resort to such tactics as deception to gain support?"

The answer, of course, is that they were using the illusion of supporting noble causes to gain political power and control. It was not until years later when I became involved—to a small degree—in the sordid world of politics that I realized just how true that was.

I was in my early thirties and employed by the Louisiana Department of Transportation and Development when I was asked by the business manager of the local state employees union to become the chairman of its newly formed Legislative Committee.

The main objective of the committee was to meet with state legislators from our districts to find ways to improve the working conditions and pay of state workers while also improving the services we provided to the citizens and visitors of the state. Although it would not bring about world peace or end poverty or hunger, I felt I had finally found a cause I could sink my teeth into, so I accepted the position. Shortly after I began my duties, I learned an important lesson: there is no better teacher in life than experience.

As I began my initial contact with the members of the state legislation, I was both surprised and encouraged by how quickly almost all of them accepted my invitations to meet with the committee. For the first time in several decades, the Louisiana government was experiencing tough economic times, and it appeared as though the people in Baton Rouge were actually interested in what the average person had to say. As it turned out, they were more interested in what the average person said about them.

Although no one from our committee notified the local press, after each meeting, reporters would inevitably be waiting outside the conference room to interview whichever legislator happened to be in attendance. These politicians were more than happy to provide the media with carefully prepared sound bites and quotable comments for the television evening news and the morning edition of the newspapers—almost none of which were based on what was actually said in the meeting itself. For an example, I will describe the events of the initial meeting, which took place at the La DOTD district headquarters in Lake Charles.

Due to scheduling conflicts, the first meeting consisted of the committee and only three members of the Southwest Louisiana Legislative Delegation. Future meetings would be held as other members became available. As per mutually agreed conditions, the meeting would start at 7:00 p.m. and last for approximately two hours. At 7:20 p.m., the last of the legislators arrived, and after a brief exchange of pleasantries, the meeting began.

I began the meeting by thanking our guests for their time and explaining why the committee had asked to meet with them. One of the representatives asked if we had any ideas on how to save the state money in the coming budget year, and I replied that we did. He then asked if I could forward a copy of those ideas to his office, got up, and said he had to leave because of a prior commitment. The other two made the same request, then got up, and left as well. The meeting was over in less than ten minutes.

As I walked out of the conference room door, I saw the first politician being interviewed by a local television reporter. His account of the meeting on camera was by far longer than what he said during the meeting. He spent about twelve minutes stating how the labor force of the state had his full and unconditional support and how proud he was to be a part of this lengthy and productive discussion designed to help put the state back on track.

After the politicians finished spewing their rhetoric and left the building, the TV camera turned my way. Still in a state of confusion over what had just happened, I responded to the reporter's questions as best I could. After the interview was over, I asked the reporter how she knew about the meeting. She said that the station had received an anonymous tip that a meeting was being held here at that moment, and it was expected to end at 7:30 p.m. In short, our committee was used by skillful politicians not to help the working class, but to make themselves look good to the voters.

In spite of this disappointing first meeting, we continued to meet with all but one of the legislators with similar results. I forwarded all the requested materials to each who asked for it with no response. They wouldn't even return my phone calls.

After a couple of weeks had passed, I received a call from the only person with whom we had previously failed to schedule a meeting. He was an attorney and state senator from Lake Charles named William L. "Bill" McLeod Jr. He requested that I meet with him alone in his office instead of meeting with the entire committee. Although I found this to be a bit unorthodox, I reluctantly agreed to his terms.

When I arrived at his office, he invited me in, asked me to take a seat, then sat there for a few seconds studying me as if he were reading an opponent in a poker game. He broke his silence to ask me what my intentions and those of my committee were. I began explaining the same way I had to the others when he interrupted me and said, "Son, don't give me your party line. Just answer the question honestly."

I assured him that what I was saying wasn't a party line; it was what we were truly working for. Without realizing it at the time, I abandoned the formal tone I had started with and began speaking to him not as a senator, but man to man, which was his intent all along. He was not only listening to what I had to say but also the passion with which I said it.

He sat there listening to me while continuing to study my facial expressions and body language. Occasionally, he would ask a question or two pertinent to the topic at hand. Once I finished speaking, there came another minute of silent stare. He then stood up, looked down at me, and said, "Okay. I'll work with you. But I want to make one thing clear right from the start. If I believe your requests of me to be valid as well as helpful to this state, I will fight tooth and nail to make them happen. But if I think your requests are unreasonable and will hurt the state, I will fight against you just as hard."

Without hesitation, I stood, shook his hand, and replied, "Senator, that is all I have ever asked for." Over the next few months, Senator McLeod and I worked together on several key issues. We won some minor battles and lost a few major ones. In the political world, it is not easy to get things done without playing the game of corruption. Once a person gives into this sometimes overwhelming temptation, they lose not only their integrity but they also lose their identity as an individual trying to make a difference for their fellow man. Senator McLeod and I both believed it was better to try and occasionally fail by doing things the right way instead of selling our souls to those who would control us like puppets on a string to further agendas we didn't believe in.

Along the way, the senator taught me a great deal about the inner workings of Louisiana politics. Trust me when I say it is not a pretty sight. While it is true that some of the specific methods used in Louisiana-style politics are unique to that state, the basic rules apply throughout the country; politicians will say and do whatever it takes to obtain and keep power.

Of all the people I worked with in and out of Baton Rouge—be they state legislators, department heads, or just everyday bureaucrats—Senator McLeod was the only person I felt I could ever trust. I never heard him use a single catchphrase to sell an agenda whether the cameras were on or not. He always called it like he saw it. And most importantly, he never once broke the promise he made to me that first day in his office. Senator McLeod has since passed on, and with his passing, I fear we have seen the extinction of a breed this country desperately needs today: an honest politician. He and his kind will be missed.

After some time, the strain of working my regular job, attending three or four meetings a week, traveling to Baton Rouge to meet with politicians, or testifying before senate committees became overwhelming. I was only one man and, in the political world at least, a nobody. I believed the *powers that be* were simply too strong and corrupt for me to make any real impact. So after some serious consideration, I resigned my position as committee chairman and returned to my regular life.

After I resigned, I began to notice how often other catchphrases were being used outside the political arena. I saw them being used as effective tools in advertising, news reports, magazine articles, and in our educational system to name a few. Although it bothered me at the time, I decided to leave that fight to someone else as well. In fact, except for exercising my right to vote and being an honest hardworking citizen, I haven't done much of anything to make a difference in this country since my short stint in the political world. That is until now.

CHAPTER ONE

The Unspoken Truth

I think there is one higher office than president and I would call that patriot.

—Gary Hart

T he worst offense a patriot can commit against their country is to do nothing. Some may say the worst offense is betrayal, but let us keep in mind someone who is willing to betray their country is not a patriot to begin with.

Average Americans have become quite adept at shaking their heads when they see or hear something they believe to be wrong, unjust, or just plain stupid. They sit around wondering what the world is coming to but are usually too afraid to make an effort to change anything. Although they may express their views privately with family and close friends, they, as individuals, feel helpless to make a difference. They believe the political and social ponds known as the system have become too large and complicated. It is the fear of being swept away by the currents and drowning that prevents them from diving in.

The first step in solving any problem is to correctly identify the problem itself. This can only be done by taking a hard, honest look at the overall situation. Without taking this crucial first step, we are simply spinning our wheels. Any solutions derived from this faulty technique are destined to fail and, in most cases, only create more problems.

While I cannot speak for other countries, it is my opinion the first problem that should be addressed in the United States is, ironically, the easiest to correct. The problem I speak of is known as political correctness or PC.

While stating things in an inoffensive way is admirable at times, and I would never suggest or promote being cruel, I believe we as a society have become far too politically correct. During the course of this publication, I will be discussing many examples ranging from the seemingly harmless term *African American* to the ridiculous need those in Congress seem to have to create separate legislation to cover the so-called hate crimes.

In the interest of fairness and accuracy, I have committed countless hours to researching the facts behind the examples I will give, as well as listening to personal eyewitness accounts and to the opinions of others. I have read articles, historical accounts, news reports, blogs, and forum discussions pertinent to these topics. I felt it necessary to do so in order to formulate and present better-informed opinions. If I had simply expressed my opinions without first doing the research, my commentary would not only be nothing more than a misinformed rant but almost certainly misleading as well. It is also important to note that the accuracy of any research is only as reliable as the material available.

While it is not my intention to convince people to share my views, this entire publication is nothing more than a collection of *my* opinions. My right to express my opinions is afforded to me by the First Amendment of the Constitution of the United States of America: the freedom of speech. I believe this right (and others) is being systematically stolen from every American, in large part, due to the effects of the mind-set of political correctness. Therefore, I feel the need to write these opinions while I still have the protection of the said amendment.

If the statement I just made leaves you with the impression that this is the ranting of an extremist, please consider my next thought. If this were twenty years ago, I would have never felt the need to insert the above disclaimer to protect myself from legal actions.

As I said before, it is not my intention to brainwash people into sharing my opinions, thoughts, or ways of life. There are enough people doing that already. It is my hope and dream to convince people to take an entirely different approach. That is, to think for themselves.

PC is not just a collection of *kinder and gentler* phrases designed to avoid offending certain people. It has become a brainwashing technique designed to control people by way of how and what they think. For example, pay closer attention to how many advertisements either directly or indirectly promote the *Think Green* movement. For the purpose of this example, the question is not whether or not you agree with their views on climate change or protecting the environment.

The real questions *should* be why is it that some people feel it necessary to *tell you what to think*? Have they hidden or distorted the facts to get you to think the way they do? Are they the same people who stand to somehow profit from convincing you to believe what they say? Are they telling the truth, or feeding you propaganda to further an agenda? If you take the time to honestly investigate these questions, you may be surprised at what you find. You may also find a better solution to the problem in the process. That reason alone makes it worth the effort.

During the course of this book, I will demonstrate an alternative method of developing opinions that are not based on mainstream thought processes such as "I heard it on the news" or "That's what they said." Whether or not you agree with my opinions is irrelevant. The point is to find a better method from which to draw your *own* conclusions—whatever they may be. This method probably won't change you from a liberal to a conservative or vice versa; it will simply allow you to become better informed about the reality of the world we live in.

By the time you finish the last chapter, if you have discovered a better method of finding the truth about the claims *they* make, isn't that also worth the effort? You be the judge.

I am not a college professor, scientist, scholar, or so-called expert on any topic. As a matter of fact, I have never even been to college. For these and many other reasons, some may question my qualifications for writing this book. My response is really quite simple: I am an American.

I am an American who has gone from dirt poor to upper middle class and back again more than once; an American who has dealt equally and fairly with people from many walks of life, such as politicians, everyday workers, businessmen, movie stars, and people crossing the border whose main need at that moment was a drink of water to survive the dangerous wilderness of the high desert. I have been conned and have witnessed people being conned and have learned through time and experience to look for the signs of a con job—from the subliminal to the overt.

In short, I have learned about life and people from my own firsthand experiences, an education that simply cannot be obtained in a classroom.

For centuries, we have been hearing the opinions of, and advice from, college professors, scientists, scholars, and experts on everything from whether or not the earth is flat to diet plans that don't work. I am not suggesting that these people should be ignored, because at times, they have been wrong.

What I am saying is that we should stop the unquestioning dependency on their every word. We should stop sitting around waiting for or allowing others to tell us how and what to think or what to do. The danger of allowing a relatively small group of people to do our thinking for us is, if those leading the way are more concerned with advancing their own agendas than advancing mankind, we soon become nothing more than sheep waiting to be herded off to slaughter.

I don't profess to be the person with all the answers to life's problems. I am sure of this because I don't believe there is such a person, nor that such a person will ever exist. I believe the only way the problems of this planet can be solved is through a joint effort of all its inhabitants. We all had a hand in screwing it up, so we should all play a role in cleaning up the mess. But unlike most messes, eliminating PC from our lives can be done one person at a time. There is no need to worry about coordinating millions of people. If you lead by example, others will soon follow, not as sheep being led to the slaughter, but as individuals who have discovered the wisdom in doing so.

It's been said that if you're not part of the solution, you're part of the problem. I, like most Americans, have been guilty of this offense. As for this average American, I believe the time for me to again take the plunge into the *pond* is long overdue. It is with this thought in mind that I have decided to write this book. In doing so, for the first time in my life, I can proudly and honestly say I am a true American patriot. And if I drown, so be it. At least I will have made the effort. I believe the people of this country—and the world—are worth that effort.

CHAPTER TWO

The Cult Mentality

When all is said and done, the real citadel of strength of any community is in the hearts and minds and desires of those who dwell there.

—Everett Dirksen

The First Amendment, in addition to protecting one's right to freedom of speech, also protects a person's right to freedom of religion. While I have no desire to either criticize or promote any religious beliefs, I have chosen the *Fundamentalist Church of Jesus Christ of Latter-Day Saints,* or *FLDS,* to illustrate what I referred to in the previous chapter as the *mind-set* of PC.

I chose this particular religious organization because the members of my wife's family are either current or former members of the FLDS, which affords me a somewhat better insight to the inner workings of its ideology and leadership structure than most outsiders. Because of what I have learned, I consider the FLDS to be a prime example of how a few people can manipulate the basic beliefs of the many to promote their own corrupt agendas.

The FLDS is a breakaway sect of the Church of Jesus Christ of Latter-day Saints (LDS), which broke off from that group in the 1890s largely because of the LDS Church's renunciation of polygamy and its decision to excommunicate practitioners of plural marriage. Because of this, it is important to note that even though the FLDS and the LDS share most of the same basic religious beliefs, in other ways, they are two separate entities.

The fundamentalist Mormons who parted ways with the LDS church in the 1890s had no organization as groups until around the 1930s and did not officially establish the FLDS title until 1991.

It was in the 1930s that the leaders of the newly organized groups—commonly referred to as "The Work"—established their headquarters in what was then called Short Creek, which spanned the border between Arizona and Utah. Short Creek eventually expanded and became incorporated as the twin municipalities of Hildale, Utah, and Colorado City, Arizona. The list of communities owned and/or controlled by the FLDS has since grown to include several locations in the United States, Canada, and Mexico. One such community is a massive compound near Eldorado, Texas, known as the YFZ Ranch, which is widely believed to be the new FLDS headquarters.

In 2002, Warren Jeffs proclaimed himself as president and *prophet, seer, and revelator* of the FLDS.[1] As prophet, Warren reportedly rules the FLDS with an iron fist.[2] His rule is considered absolute by both him and the estimated ten thousand members of the church.

But with absolute power comes absolute corruption. Warren Jeffs is apparently no exception. According to some former followers, he maintains his hold even after his arrest in August 2006.

I have been told by some former members that most of the FLDS faithfuls consider the prophet to be godlike and would willingly lay down their lives for him. There are reports that some members, if asked to do so, would sacrifice themselves to carry out acts of vengeance against other members or former members for *certain sins* the prophet felt had been committed against the church or the prophet's doctrine. This practice is known within the FLDS as blood atonement.

Blood atonement was originally a ritual where the sinner would willingly kneel on the ground and lean forward allowing someone to come from behind and slit his/her throat. In doing so, this *spilling of blood on the ground* would atone for their sins, thereby ensuring the sinner a place in heaven.

This ritual was suspected to have been carried out mainly during the early years of Brigham Young, but some former FLDS members I have spoken with claim that Warren has been known to preach of returning to this practice. Many of those former members suspect that if Warren were to return to the practice, the modern version would not be limited to the willing. But to date, I have found no credible evidence that any blood atonements have actually taken place within the FLDS.

Whether the practice of blood atonements are revived or not, the mere threat of its use can be used as a powerful psychological tool in maintaining control over FLDS members past and present.

Warren's ambitious rise to power and corrupt hunger to control his followers has been well documented since the raid on the YFZ Ranch conducted by Texas authorities in April 2008.

In an article published on March 5, 2009, entitled "Listening to the Lord: Jeffs exerted 24-7 control over FLDS faithful," Brooke Adams, who covers polygamy for the *Salt Lake Tribune*, wrote,[3]

> *As he crisscrossed the country eluding arrest, polygamous sect leader Warren S. Jeffs wielded control over an inner circle of believers to a startling degree.*

> *From the mundane to the intimate—trading in a four-wheeler, having heart surgery, arranging marriages and naming babies—few aspects of life escaped his scrutiny and say.*

> *Jeffs controlled time and physical environments. He formed and destroyed personal relationships. He created new identities for his followers. He fanned fear with apocalyptic predictions and cultivated powerlessness with loss of salvation. He used rewards and punishments to modify behavior and shut down criticism.*

> *Jeffs, president of the Fundamentalist Church of Jesus Christ of Latter-Day Saints, did it with a simple claim: The Lord was directing his every move.*

> *The details of how Jeffs exercised this control—mostly over his large family and those of hand-picked members sent to a remote Texas ranch—are contained in pages of his daily diary. The entries are included as exhibits in a court proceeding and released as public documents by San Angelo, Texas, Judge Barbara Walther.*

Adams, after pointing out that Warren dictates his thoughts to a scribe, later speaks of his continued influence and quotes a Utah state official:

> *Jeffs, who has led the sect since 2002, has never spoken publicly about alleged illegal activities or state actions targeting him or his community.*

> *But the dictations show "a day-to-day, ongoing control of people's lives that was extraordinary," said Utah Attorney General Mark Shurtleff, who has reviewed them. "He had absolute control over his people."*

> *That has lessened since Jeffs' arrest and conviction, though his followers remain devoted to him.*

Jeffs, like prophets before him, maintains control over his flock by creating an atmosphere of *us against them*. He convinced his followers they needed his guidance and wisdom to protect themselves against those in the wicked world who seek to do them harm.

As part of church doctrine, the FLDS believes in and allows *faithful priesthood* men to have multiple wives. However, due to state and federal laws, they may only legally marry one. So in a religious ceremony, other wives are *sealed* to their husbands without public record. The FLDS also believe that men should father as many children with their wives as possible.

To avoid detection by government officials of the secondary marriages and the offspring these marriages produce, it had been a common practice in the past to list a fictitious father's name on a child's birth certificate, although this practice doesn't appear to be as common today.

How does one man come to command such power over so many people? Is it simply religious zealotry that causes people to allow someone to have that much control over them? I believe it is attributable to the ability of an individual or individuals to manipulate the strong religious beliefs of others to serve their own needs through fear, intimidation, and sometimes even love.

My wife, Susannah, is the seventh of nine children born to Elaine Jeffs. Elaine is Rulon Jeffs's eldest daughter and Warren Jeffs's half sister. She was the second of six concurrent wives to Susannah's father, Wilford A. Draper. Along with the children born to the other five wives, plus those born to his first wife who divorced him on learning of his decision to join the FLDS, Susannah has a total of thirty-five full and/or half siblings. She was born in Salt Lake City, Utah, thirteen years before her grandfather, Rulon Jeffs, became the FLDS leader and prophet. Susannah would not stay in the FLDS long enough to see that event take place first hand. At age eleven, she was rescued from the sect during what I consider to be a courageous act of selfless devotion.

Elaine, who had grown increasingly disenchanted with life in the FLDS and its doctrine, convinced Wilford to allow her to attend university night classes in order to advance her career at the University of Utah Hospital. In fact, as she later came to realize, she was really looking for a way out. On July 4, 1982, she moved out of the family home into an apartment so she could have a quiet place to study away from the distractions of a house filled with so many people. Ironically, that was her personal Independence Day.

Through her exposure to the outside world, she gained the knowledge, experience, and courage to finally break free from her fundamentalist roots. Even though she was born into it and had considered leaving the FLDS for some time, it was still a very difficult decision for her make. She knew that to have any chance of being successful, she would have to do the one thing, which is arguably the hardest for a mother to do; she would have to leave her children behind. But she also knew it would be for only a while.

By the end of 1982, Wilford began to suspect something wasn't quite right. He saw changes in Elaine's behavior inconsistent with the teachings of the church. Sometime in the beginning of 1983, her visits with her children became more guarded by Wilford. Over the next fifteen to eighteen months, the visits began to resemble those of divorcing couples engaged in a messy custody battle. They became less frequent, and eventually, Wilford forbade the children from visiting their mother at all.

Elaine knew something had to be done. After consulting with attorneys and state officials as to her legal rights regarding custody of her children, she devised a plan.

In June 1984, she arranged a visit at a local McDonald's restaurant with eight of her nine children, two of whom were already of legal age and were in on the plan. (The ninth another adult son, was out of town at the time.) Also attending this visit was Wilford and two of Susannah's half brothers. Around the corner from the order counter, they chose a table where Elaine's eldest son's role was to keep his father engaged in conversation while she took five of her six minor children along with Anne, her eldest daughter, to the order counter. Unfortunately, her sixteen-year-old son, Samuel, chose to stay at the table with his father. While Elaine placed the order, Anne fulfilled her role of escorting her younger siblings out the opposite side door to the family van. Elaine had previously instructed Anne to leave her behind and drive the children safely away if it became necessary.

As food was being placed on the counter, one of the half brothers came around the corner to assist with bringing their orders back to the table and discovered his siblings being hurried out the door. Upon seeing him, Elaine quickly tossed more than enough money on the counter, grabbed as many bags of food as she could, and ran out to the van. Anne drove her mother and the children to a rental car Elaine had previously hidden nearby.

As planned, Anne returned the van to the restaurant and was to walk back to her father's home to retrieve her vehicle and go home. However, her half brothers saw her leaving the van; she was chased down and taken back in the van along with the rest of the family left at the restaurant. In the rental car, Elaine drove her five minor children to an undisclosed location.

When Anne got back, she motioned for Samuel to get in her car, but before she could drive away, one of Wilford's wives let the air out of one tire to prevent her from leaving. Samuel was ordered out of her car and into the house. He complied.

Because she was being held and harassed by her father, Anne called the police who then talked to her father, advising him he could not force her to stay since she was a legally married adult. She was then allowed to go after using a bicycle pump to put enough air into her tire to get her to a service station.

Samuel was not allowed to leave with her. Helen, the eldest daughter of the then minor children, eventually returned to her father's home. Both Samuel and Helen are, by choice, still living inside the cult today.

As part of FLDS practice, children belong only to their priesthood-bearing fathers who are considered proverbial lords of their castles. In the simplest terms, wives are merely expected to tend to the children's day-to-day needs, much like nannies, in addition to rendering strict obedience to their husbands.

Because of advancing ill health, Wilford had become dependent on Elaine's income to support his family. While there is no way to know for sure, I believe Wilford realized he had lost much of his control over Elaine and used her children to prevent losing total control and the income she provided. If so, he underestimated the one thing that he counted on to hold the family together, but instead would eventually lead to the undoing of his plan: a mother's love.

At this point, you may be asking yourself what this story has to do with political correctness. Although some may disagree, I view political correctness as one crucial method used by people who wish to manipulate the basic beliefs of those they wish to control. They do so by inventing alternative catchphrases to common public perceptions in order to distract, and eventually alter people's opinions and beliefs to suit their own agendas. This method is at least unethical and, at worst, brainwashing.

In order to maintain purpose for their way of life, members of the FLDS are constantly reminded they are *God's chosen few*—the only ones God will save from destruction during the coming apocalypse. Although this concept is not unique to the FLDS, it is ingrained as one of their strongest beliefs and is therefore a driving force in how they conduct themselves in their everyday lives.

When Elaine decided to remove her children from the FLDS, she had two options. She could go through the legal system with her claims based on an illegal polygamous marriage, or she could attempt the rescue. As you have seen, she chose the latter. Why did she make that choice? First, she felt dragging her family through a messy custody battle would be too harmful for everyone involved. Secondly, she knew the ramifications of going against the rules of the powerful leaders of the church. She realized that she and her children would be at the mercy of leaders who wielded complete control over their followers.

In Elaine's mind, nothing was out of bounds when it came to retribution, not even blood atonement. Wilford would often remind Elaine and her "sister wives" of a story he had heard about an LDS member in the 1800s who had caught his wife cheating on him and exercised his priesthood right to blood atonement by shooting her to death. He also told them that he believed that killing was justified because the husband saved her soul, and she would therefore be with him in the next life. Although no actual threat was ever specifically directed at her, Elaine believed Wilford was sending her and her sister wives a message that if they ever broke their wedding vows, they could suffer the same fate.

Whether the story Wilford told was true or not is irrelevant for the purpose of this example. By repeatedly telling the story, Wilford instilled the perceived threat to her life into Elaine's consciousness. She believed running was the best chance she and her children had in order to be safe. It is difficult to hurt those you cannot find.

If you require further evidence of how the FLDS uses PC to control their followers, I submit the following for your consideration.

There are some who believe blood atonement justifies the *spilling of blood on the ground* by claiming it is carried out with love and compassion for the sinner, not out of vengeance. The intention is to *save the sinner.* Committing murder against people who do things you don't agree with and then assigning a seemingly *holy* title to such actions in an attempt to justify the crime is placing quite a spin on reality.

Political correctness, in essence, does the same thing. While the FLDS may be considered an extreme case in point, we are all being indoctrinated by such catchphrases and mind control on a daily basis—usually without realizing how much.

Chapter Three

What's In A Name?

You can call a puppy a purebred all you wish, but that won't stop it from peeing on the carpet.

—Ron Walker

T o understand the dangers of political correctness, we must first properly identify what it is all about. There are those who see PC as nothing more than a collection of polite phrases designed to eliminate the possibility of offending others. They also believe by using PC terminology, they will help close the gap between different ethnic groups, genders, and religious groups. PC goes much further into the human psyche than mere politeness or human harmony. I believe it can also do the opposite; it can actually help widen gaps between people.

Webster defines *being politically correct* as[4] "conforming to a belief that language and practices which could offend political sensibilities (as in matters of sex or race) should be eliminated—political correctness *noun*."

Another definition of PC is one I found on Wikipedia's website, which states,[5]

> *Political correctness (adjectivally, politically correct; both forms commonly abbreviated to PC) is a term applied to language, ideas, policies, or behavior seeking to conform to authority or orthodox thought. Usually this term is used in a sarcastic way to imply or ridicule the authority or thought as unquestionable or authoritative beyond discussion. Conversely, the term "politically incorrect" is used to refer to language or ideas that may cause offense or that are unconstrained by orthodoxy.*

Whichever definition you choose, you will find one common denominator: PC is a form of mind control.

Listed below is a small sampling of words or phrases that have been used in the past and their more commonly used PC counterparts:

- *broken home*: Dysfunctional family
- *criminal*: Unsavory character, behaviorally challenged.
- *bum*: Homeless person
- *black person*: African American
- *congressman*: Congressperson
- *Christmas tree*: Holiday tree
- *crazy*: Mentally challenged
- *failure*: Deferred success
- *fat*: Obese, calorically enhanced.
- *bald*: Follically challenged
- *garbage man*: Sanitation engineer
- *ghetto*: Economically disadvantaged area
- *handicapped*: Physically challenged
- *merry Christmas*: Happy holidays, season's greetings.
- *housewife*: Domestic engineer, home decorator.
- *illegal alien*: Undocumented worker/migrant/immigrant, day laborer, guest worker, freedom worker.
- *janitor*: Custodial artist, sanitation engineer.
- *lazy*: Motivationally challenged
- *man's job/woman's work*: Traditional gender role
- *midget*: Vertically challenged, little people
- *natural disaster*: Unnatural event
- *old people*: Senior citizens
- *punishment*: Time out
- *secretary*: Administrative assistant
- *sex change*: Gender reassignment
- *slum*: Economic oppression zone
- *stupid*: Intellectually impaired
- *ugly*: Visually challenging

According to PC terminology, I would be considered a height-enhanced, calorically-challenged, follically-challenged, pigment-challenged male who is also facially follically enhanced. Obviously, that description is quite a mouthful. In fact, I am a tall slender bald white guy with a beard.

Those who practice PC would prefer to use the first description so as to not offend me by using the second. I would not be offended by either, quite frankly; but I do find the PC description rather silly. I do own mirrors and am therefore well aware of my appearance. While I, like most people, wish some of my features were different, I am happy with the way I look overall. I tend to adopt the Popeye mentality of "I yam what I yam."

So what is the big deal about using these terms? At face value, there is nothing wrong with them. After all, I would never tell someone they were fat and ugly. That would simply be rude. If someone who fit that description were to ask my opinion, I would probably tell them they were overweight or heavyset and average or plain looking. It is the desire most people have not to be cruel or insensitive to others, which makes PC such an effective brainwashing technique.

However, I find it impossible to view a rapist or murderer as *behaviorally challenged* or a child molester as a mere *unsavory character*. I would refer to them as what they truly are: criminals. Using PC terms in these cases diminishes and mocks the pain of the victims and their loved ones. I would not want to be the district attorney who had to tell the parents of a four-year-old child who had just been brutally, sexually assaulted by a pedophile that a conviction is unlikely because the *unsavory character* who committed this offense is considered to be *behaviorally challenged*. If you think this is an extreme example, read a newspaper. Defense attorneys will use any and every PC term they can think of to make the crimes their clients commit seem less severe to the jury.

Let's take the case of the infamous *Twinkie defense*[6] as an example. On November 27, 1978, Dan White, a former San Francisco City supervisor, shot and killed Mayor George Moscone and City Supervisor Harvey Milk. White was arrested and charged with first-degree murder in connection with the killings. In order to convict the accused of first-degree murder in California, prosecutors must, by law, prove premeditation.

Contrary to popular belief, the actual legal defense White's lawyers used was called diminished capacity. White's defense team never claimed "Twinkies made him do it," as it was widely reported in the press. They instead claimed White's actions were the result of the depressed mental state from which he was then suffering, although much of the testimony given suggested the *Twinkie defense* was the true motivation.

White, who had previously been a fitness fanatic and health food advocate, had begun consuming junk food and sugar-laden soft drinks. His lawyers, through testimony given by noted psychiatrist Martin Blinder, claimed his change in diet was one of the many symptoms of his depression. Blinder also testified about theories that excessive sugar consumption could have aggravated a chemical imbalance in White's brain that may have worsened his mood swings. George Solomon,[7] another psychiatrist who testified on behalf of the defense, reportedly said White had "exploded" and was "sort of on automatic pilot" when he killed the two men.

According to testimony given at the trial, on the day of the murders, White, who was carrying a loaded gun, crawled through a basement window at the city hall to avoid metal detectors. He then sneaked past Moscone's bodyguards, went into the mayor's office, and demanded he be reinstated to the position from which he (White) had previously resigned. When Moscone refused, White shot him twice at close range, then stood over the body and shot him twice more in the head to make sure the mayor was indeed dead. He then reloaded his weapon and went down the hall where he found and shot Harvey Milk five times. That sounds like a pretty well thought-out and premeditated plan to me.

In spite of this evidence, and in part due to the testimony given by the psychiatrists, White's lawyers were successful in presenting their diminished capacity defense. The jury found White's capacity for rational thought had been diminished, thereby incapable of the premeditation required for a murder conviction. Instead, he was convicted of voluntary manslaughter.

Many people believe the diminished capacity defense was designed to relieve people like Dan White of much if not all the responsibility for their actions in the minds of a jury. I tend to agree. Apparently, so did the California State Legislature. In 1982, by way of Proposition 8, the term *diminished capacity* was abolished.[8] It was replaced with *diminished actuality*, referring to whether or not the accused actually had the required intent to commit the crime for which they were charged.

This is a prime example of how PC works as well as how it can be used to control thought. If the word *capacity* had not been in the old law, perhaps White would have been convicted on the original charge, as I believe he should have been.

Replacing the word *capacity* with *actuality* changes the meaning of the term, which means it could be seen as reverse PC. In this case, however, I must admit I do agree with the change, but only because it was done to better reflect the original intent of the law and to remove any politically correct loopholes. Hopefully, more legal loopholes designed to relieve criminals of responsibility for their actions will be closed in the future.

PC terms are not only used to create legal loopholes for people like Dan White but they can also be used to create loopholes and sympathy for the less fortunate.

Some people who support PC cringe when they hear the term *illegal alien*—a term used to describe anyone who is in the United States without proper authorization. In short, it identifies people who are in this country illegally. The term elicits a mental image of poor, oppressed Mexicans who risk everything to come to the United States and, as the PC people put it, "do the jobs Americans don't want," such as migrant farmworkers and maids. That assumption is only partly correct.

Although it is true most of the illegal aliens in this country do come here from Mexico, there are also people from all over the world who are here illegally, and they—Mexican nationals or otherwise—are no longer limiting their lines of work to just our farms and kitchens. Go to almost any medium to large-sized construction site and you might be surprised. You will find many jobs that were once held by hardworking Americans are now being contracted out to companies that almost exclusively hire illegal aliens. This problem is not limited only to the construction industry.

The service industry, which includes such businesses as restaurants, car washes, carpet cleaning companies, and others, have all been inundated to varying degrees by people who are in this country illegally. In fact, in the states that border Mexico, it is becoming increasingly difficult to find places of business that do not employ illegal aliens; and this situation is quickly spreading to neighboring states as well. While I do have compassion for most of these people and have a great deal of respect for their desire to make a better life for themselves and their families, what they, and the companies that hire them, are doing is placing a greater burden on an already strained national economy.

As of 2010, there were an estimated twelve to twenty million illegal aliens in the United States, and these figures are expected to grow dramatically each year. Even if you exclude the "jobs Americans don't want" and the children of those here illegally, there are still several million jobs that are being filled by illegal aliens who, by definition, are breaking the law by being here in the first place. Imagine how much better off our economy would be if only half of those jobs were filled by tax-paying, home-owning Americans. In these troubled times of recession, inflation, government bailouts, high fuel prices, and near record-breaking unemployment rates, we can no longer afford to ignore this ever-increasing problem. Why then do we? Because it is politically correct to do so.

PC people, through a sense of their own compassion, have developed a new set of PC terms to describe illegal aliens. They use terms such as *undocumented worker/migrant/immigrant*, *day laborer*, *guest worker*, and my personal favorite, *freedom worker*. These terms are often used in an attempt to divert attention from the fact illegal aliens are violating a multitude of our laws.

I must remember that the next time I get pulled over for speeding and simply inform the officer I should not be issued a citation because I was only speeding to prevent being late for work. I would further explain that without my job, I would be unable to provide a better way of life for my family, and because of that, I should be excused for violating any traffic laws. Besides, it would be politically incorrect to issue a ticket to a *freedom driver*. If I have the opportunity to test this before this goes to print, I promise to let you know how much the ticket cost me as well as how long the officer laughed in my face.

Most PC people have a very naive concept of the severity of the problem we as a nation now face because of illegal immigration. They hear stories on the news of illegal factory workers being rounded up and deported. Then they hear reports of home foreclosures at record levels with no clues to the connection between the two. It's quite simple really: if American home owners are getting squeezed out of jobs by illegal aliens, where will they find the money to pay their mortgages?

And let's not forget the increased strain being placed on our social services. A large number of illegal aliens, due to their undocumented status, don't pay income taxes but are entitled to benefits such as free health care, free public education, and many other services taxpaying Americans pay for. Others obtain work and these benefits by using falsified documents, sometimes by way of identity theft.

With the large number of American jobs that have already been outsourced overseas, American workers have been forced to redefine their roles in the workplace. Because we are currently involved in that highly sensitive transitional process, we can ill afford being forced to compete for the remaining jobs with people who, legally, have no right to be here. In spite of this, legislation was introduced during the George W. Bush administration to grant amnesty to illegal aliens who have been in this country for a designated period. Similar legislation is now being considered by President Obama.

Obama's plan is technically not outright amnesty, although it realistically amounts to the same thing. Under his proposal of *comprehensive immigration reform,* those who are already in this country illegally would be provided with a *path to citizenship* by paying a $500 fine and also paying back taxes on the income they have made while working under undocumented status. According to the president, this plan would bring in more tax revenue to the treasury and allow millions of people who are now hiding from authorities to *come out of the shadows.* Here we have a trifecta of PC rhetoric all in one plan that will create more problems than it will solve.

Instead of adding to the problem, would it not make more sense to simply enforce the laws that are currently on the books by investigating and imposing fines on employers who hire illegal aliens? Although I am against the overall practice of corporate outsourcing of American jobs overseas, an additional solution to the illegal immigration problem would be to ask American companies that insist on outsourcing to do so in the countries that have the largest numbers of their population in the United States illegally.

For example, most of the illegal aliens I have met are from Mexico. Almost every one of them I have spoken to has told me they would love nothing more than to be working at home in their own country where they can be near their families and friends. But they cannot do so without jobs there, which is why they are in this country. If American companies would set up factories and shops in Mexico, it would not only help alleviate the problem here, but at the same time, it would also improve the economy of our neighbors to the south. In the interest of fairness, some companies have done just that, though their numbers are still far too few.

And what about the economy of the United States? As it is now, millions of illegal aliens are sending money out of the United States each month to help support their families back home. That relates to billions of dollars that are not being placed back into our economy. With the American economy in the worst shape it has been since the Great Depression, this too is a situation we can ill afford.

An article written for the Federation for American Immigration Reform (FAIR)—last updated in July 2009—sheds some light on just how much money is being sent to other countries:[9]

> *In 2006, the Inter-American Development Bank (IDB) reported that remittances received by Latin American and Caribbean countries had climbed in 2008 to a total of nearly $70 billion. This amount was triple the amount received in 2001.*
>
> *Remittances provide temporary financial relief at the household level and increase foreign exchange earnings*

*for the receiving country, but they also have an equal
negative effect on the balance of payments of the sending
country.*

*For Mexico, remittances are an important source of income.
Mexicans living in the United States sent a record $23.1
billion back home in 2006, putting remittances third
after oil and maquiladora (assembly plant) exports as a
foreign-exchange generator for Mexico. Current IDB data
indicate that the level of remittances received in Mexico
had risen to $25.1 billion in 2008.*

This information could also shed some light on why Mexican officials are so reluctant to secure their side of the U.S. border while criticizing efforts made by states like Arizona who pass legislation to deal with illegal immigration problems. Apparently, it solves two major economic problems for them: (1) it is a major source of income, (2) there are now twelve to twenty million fewer people in their country for them to worry about.

Using U.S. Census Bureau figures, one study has concluded that the population of immigrants, legal and illegal, in the United States is currently rising at an estimated net of 1.25 million per year.[10] At that rate of growth, there will be an estimated 105 million illegal aliens by 2060, with one in every three being here illegally. If you do the math, it doesn't take long to figure out this economic problem will become increasingly worse with each passing year.

Politically correct minded people, like most of us, have no problem screaming bloody murder when our government spends billions of dollars to bail out mismanaged major corporations. Even though many Americans disagree with this practice, it is important to remember that these companies are still major contributors to our economy. They provide thousands of American jobs, income tax revenue generated by those jobs, and tax revenue on the sales of their products. Although it may take years to do so, eventually, we as taxpayers usually get back all the monies spent on bailouts.

However, when it comes to the problem of revenue forever lost to the people of the United States by illegal aliens, these same politically correct minded individuals are either too naive to recognize the problem, or choose to sweep the problem under the rug and pretend it doesn't exist. Either way, I believe we as a nation can no longer afford to ignore this dangerous economic problem simply to avoid offending those responsible.

Companies that hire people who do not wish to have their legal status known do so for one reason: cheap labor. If the amnesty legislation were to pass, these companies will still pay their now legal employees a low wage as they did before, but without fear of being fined or sent to prison for hiring an illegal employee—not that they have much to worry about now. The only advantage to the worker is having legal status. However, they will all have to pay income tax like the rest of us. Although having legal status is obviously a major plus for the employee, who really benefits from this plan?

Anyone who has worked on a construction site in the past fifteen years is well aware of the increased importance placed on safety on the job site. You are told to report any and all unsafe working conditions and reminded to always wear the proper safety equipment (gloves, safety glasses, hard hats, etc.). Any violation of these regulations is usually dealt with swiftly with punishment ranging from a simple verbal warning to termination of employment depending on the severity and frequency of the offense. I have only seen two exceptions to this rule. The first is when the client or contractor is losing large sums of money due to work being behind schedule. The second is with certain violations involving illegal aliens.

Even with all the emphasis placed on safety, construction sites are still inherently dangerous. Workers are usually always aware that no matter how much they collectively try to avoid them, accidents still occur. While hard work is expected, clients, contractors, and workers all agree working too hard or too fast dramatically increases the chances of such accidents. A steady but safe pace is therefore recommended.

The overwhelming majority of the illegal aliens who work in the construction field are honest, hardworking people. Whether it is due to threats made by their employers or mere assumption on their part, illegal workers are constantly haunted by the knowledge that if terminated, they can easily be replaced by scores of others who would gladly take their place. This situation creates a constant motivation for these workers to work at an almost superhuman pace. It also places not only themselves but also everyone around them at a greatly increased risk of injury or death.

With that in mind, we should all take a hard, honest look at the effects PC has had on this situation. In an effort to *help* these workers by making it socially unacceptable to even use the term *illegal aliens*, has political correctness really helped their plight, or has it done more harm than good? How can we properly and accurately address this issue if even the mere mention of it has become so taboo?

Instead of making the tough decisions that would bring this nation out of economic hardship, our political leaders have chosen to give in to the trap of political correctness for their own or their political party's agendas. But why wouldn't they? After all, if the amnesty legislation with its low-cost path to citizenship giving the newly empowered *freedom worker* the right to vote passes, there would be another twenty million votes for those who push it through. So again I ask, who really benefits here?

As I said before, I am not unsympathetic to the plight of those who come here to escape the poverty and corruption of their homelands to make a better life. I can and do hold the governments of those countries responsible for the depressed economic states of their nations that forces people to leave their homeland, their friends, and in a large number of cases, their families behind in order to support their loved ones.

I also hold responsible those politicians in this country who use PC rhetoric to take advantage of these people by using them as political pawns for political gain.

In the past, when the economy of the United States was strong enough to support a much smaller number of illegal aliens, I too looked the other way. But the simple truth is, if we continue to do so, one day we will find *ourselves* a third-world nation. Then *we* will be the ones looking toward some other country to start a new life; and all for the benefit of political gain, big business, and for the sake of being politically correct? For me, the price is far too high.

CHAPTER FOUR

Sharing The
Big Blue Marble
(AKA Earth)

An individual has not started living until he can rise above the narrow confines of his individualistic concerns to the broader concerns of all humanity.

—Martin Luther King, Jr.

After reading the previous chapter, many of you have probably dubbed me a racist. If so, your opinion will most likely not improve after reading this chapter. If you take the time to honestly think about what I have said and what I am about to say, you may find I am not speaking of a hatred of races other than mine. On the contrary, I am speaking of equality and fairness for all people.

What country illegal aliens come from or what they look like is of no importance to me. My only concern is the effect they are having on the economy of this nation and the people living and working here legally. You may have noticed I did not limit the last statement to American citizens only. There are millions of immigrants, most who are not yet or may never become American citizens, living and working in this country legally. Those who are here legally usually come from the same countries as illegal aliens. I don't have a problem with individuals who are in this country legally, nor do I blame the individuals who are here illegally. I cannot blame illegal aliens for wanting to make a better life for themselves and their families. After all, don't most of us want exactly the same thing?

While there are some restrictions and exceptions, most legal aliens—those without citizen status—are subject to the same rules, regulations, and laws as the rest of us. They basically receive the same pay and benefits for the same work as their citizen counterparts. When illegal aliens are hired at much lower wages, often with little or no benefits, it reduces the overall level of wage standards and working conditions, which so many Americans have fought so long and hard to obtain. With the exception of big business and our political leaders, this practice creates an unfair situation for everyone involved.

Political correctness also preys on the inherent desire we as humans have to fit into society. Whether it is in our nature to do so or strictly for the purpose of fitting into society, most people tend to follow the so-called Golden Rule, which states, "Do unto others as you would have them do unto you." Unfortunately, there are also many people who have adopted the mentality of "do as I say, not as I do." A case in point would be the ongoing debate over the Miss Black America pageant.

Let me state for the record that I have absolutely no interest in *any* beauty pageant whatsoever. With the exception of the advancement of the free enterprise system, and having doors opened to the winners in the form of fame and scholarships, I find *all* beauty pageants to be boring and a complete waste of time. I would not, however, advocate the elimination of beauty pageants. In addition to the reasons given above, they do seem to be a good source of entertainment for those who enjoy them. As for me, I can always change the channel.

Although there are several ethnically based beauty pageants, I have chosen the Miss Black America pageant because it is the most well known, and I consider it the best example for making my point.

On August 17, 1968, the first Miss Black America pageant was held in Philadelphia, Pennsylvania. It was originally created and produced by J. Morris Anderson as a local area pageant and as a protest of the exclusion of black women in the Miss America pageant. With strong support from Phillip H. Savage, the tri-state director of the NAACP at that time, the pageant brought a great deal of attention to this problem through nationwide press coverage. It is widely believed this protest was responsible for the eventual acceptance of black women into the Miss America pageant in 1970.

Since then, several states have had black women as their representatives in the Miss America pageant and seven black women have won the title. In 1990, Debbye Turner won the Miss America crown and was followed in 1991 by Marjorie Judith Vincent, thus becoming the first pair of black women to win back-to-back titles. Why then does the Miss Black America pageant still exist? While I am not an expert on beauty pageants, I believe there are two main reasons: money and self-segregation.

Although the popularity of beauty pageants in general has declined in the past decade, they still generate a great deal of revenue. Thousands of girls and young women apply to enter pageants each year. Most, if not all, pay a nonrefundable application fee. Those fees, in addition to corporate sponsorships, contributions from private and civil groups, and revenue from the television networks, which broadcast the events, can leave the more popular pageants with hefty bank accounts. Even though some pageants are officially classified as nonprofit organizations, they still relate to big business. That makes them too profitable for the producers and organizers to simply walk away.

In the case of ethnically based pageants, I believe the second reason I mentioned, self-segregation, falls most accurately under my subject matter. Again, I will use the Miss Black America pageant debate to make my point.

After reading a great deal of material and getting varied points of view on both sides of the discussion, I went to the MBA website to see what it had to say. I found it in process of being updated, so I was initially only able to view the main splash page as well as an information page with a link to the registration form for the local competition in the Washington DC, Maryland, and Northern Virginia areas. I eventually found links to some of the new pages under construction as well as a link to the History page of the old site.

To illustrate what is widely believed to be true (the MBA pageant being originally intended as a protest against the exclusion of black women in the Miss America pageant), we need only read the first paragraph of the History page of the old site:[11]

> From the time J. Morris Anderson first created and produced the Miss Black America Pageant on August 17, 1968 until the present, there has always been one major question asked: Why should there be a Miss Black America Pageant since there is already a Miss America Pageant? Always, the answer has been: "To provide a forum for the Black Man to say his wife is mentally, spiritually, and physically beautiful the same as the white man has a forum through which to say his woman is beautiful." The MBA Pageant has always provided a stage on which the Black woman could display her talent; a platform on which she

could air her views; and, a pedestal from where she could
reign as a universal symbol of pride and dignity.

Was this act of self-segregating protest necessary in the turbulent times of 1968? In principle, I believe it was. Not only were there prejudices from people in the white community against black people but there were also prejudices against the shades of skin color within the black community itself. Unfortunately, both prejudices still exist to this day. Again, I refer to the old MBA website:

The MBA Pageant was created more as a protest against the negative self images that Black people imposed upon themselves than against the powers which imposed those images. The fact is that many Black mothers once pinched the noses of their young in attempts to cause them to have narrow, Caucasian features. Many forced their children to walk around with clothes pins squeezing their noses to acquire narrow features. And many Black youth yet hear their parents talking about the pretty little girl or handsome little boy with the "good" hair and the "light skin." This old, stereotypical thinking is what caused and yet causes Blacks to think that curly hair is bad and dark skin with African features is ugly. These negative attitudes yet remain prevalent in America. Therefore, there remains a need for the Miss Black America Pageant to stay alive and continue its work.

After visiting the MBA website, I reread the comments made by both sides of the debate, and again carefully considered all points of view. The comments struck at something that had been nagging me in the back of my mind for years, although exactly what that was remained unclear. So I read the material a third time, but this time, I decided to read between the lines.

I realized there was far more being said about the current state of race relations in this country than how it relates to a mere beauty pageant. To accurately explain what I mean by that, I must again give you a small sample of my personal history and experiences.

I was born in Louisiana in the fall of 1960 and spent my first forty years in numerous places throughout the South. For reasons unrelated to the subject of this book, I have often felt I was born at the wrong time in human history. But I also believe things happen for a reason. During the sixties and early seventies, I witnessed one of the most historic and turbulent periods in American history.

In addition to many other notable events, I watched the space race and the eventual first visit to the moon, the Vietnam War, and the assassinations of President John F. Kennedy, Senator Robert Kennedy, and civil rights leader Martin Luther King Jr. I also witnessed the heart of the civil rights movement and the effect it had on the people of this nation. To say my most impressionable years were a time of great change would be a gross understatement. In retrospect, perhaps growing up in that era gave me a unique perspective as to the progress as well as mistakes we as a society have made since then.

I was seven years old when the first Miss Black America pageant was held. I can still hear the reactions to this event by other white people I knew. It is safe to say those views were widely shared by the majority of the white community throughout the country. I heard comments made such as "A black beauty pageant? What is beautiful about being black?" Or, "Well, that's good. We don't want them in our pageant anyway!"

In addition to the research I did on the Internet, I also spoke with several people—black and white—about this topic. The responses I received face-to-face were typical of those I read online. The comments made by most black people were insightful and thought-provoking. Unfortunately, many dismissed me as a racist for even asking the question. This response was also common with whites who agree with and promote the PC mind-set. I also heard from some black people, saying, "It's a black thing. You wouldn't understand."

While I find the last response to be closed minded because of the intent of its use, there is some truth to that statement. Each of us can intellectually conceptualize the pain felt when we hear a friend's parent has died. But it was not until my own father passed away that I fully understood the grief one feels. If you have never been in combat, you can never fully understand the horrors of war. If you are not a woman, you can never fully understand how a woman feels. If you are not a black person in America, you can never fully understand the black American experience. If you are not a white person in America, you can never fully understand the way white people in America think.

With that in mind, I took another look at the question most asked by white people during the course of my research: "Why do we still need a Miss Black America pageant?" At that moment, I realized what had been nagging me in the back of my mind all those years: something had changed and it had changed in a big way. I believe the most important part of that question is missed by most: *still need*. This, in my opinion, shows a huge shift in the overall attitude of whites in regard to racism in this country.

The overwhelming majority of white people I spoke with denounced the highly racist attitudes, which were so prevalent in 1968. They see racism in general as a useless waste of time and energy. Although racism is not exclusive to differences between whites and blacks, most white people see the civil rights movement as the struggle black people (and some white people) fought, and continue to fight, to gain an overall equality in America.

The white people who question the existence of different beauty pageants are not being racist. What they are really asking is, "Haven't we grown past the need for them in today's society?" They feel that if it was wrong for the Miss America pageant to be segregated, then it is equally wrong for any pageant.

Therefore, when white people see minorities continuing to engage in self-segregating activities such as ethnically based beauty pageants, it is not the activities themselves, but the seemingly double standards practiced by those minorities who have fought so hard to obtain racial unity and equality. The "do as I say and not as I do" mentality is one we *all* hated to hear from our parents when we were children. As adults, it still leaves a bad taste.

Does this mean there are no longer any white racists? No. There are still white people who believe in the supreme superiority of the white race and preach stereotypical ideals. Other whites have instead chosen to invoke and support new stereotypes. Does this mean there are no black racists? No. There are those in the black community who still promote the stereotypical idea that all white people are racists. Some of the more radical factions support segregation of blacks from whites in almost all areas of society. Doesn't that sound familiar?

Fortunately, however, most of the black people I spoke with recognize the basic differences between the racism that continues today and the attitudes of those of years past. They also recognize that while we as a society still have a great deal of work to do, there has been a great deal of progress made—as do the white people asking, "Why do we *still need* separate beauty pageants? Does this mean we should forget our history and pretend it never happened?" Absolutely not.

Let's remember, those who forget history are doomed to repeat it. At the same time, those who dwell in the past are doomed to remain stuck there forever. Instead of dwelling in the past, we should continue to learn from those mistakes and work together as the *human race* to correct the problems that still remain today. I believe we can achieve this goal and still maintain a peaceful and proud celebration of our unique cultures and heritages.

It doesn't always take events such as beauty pageants to create self-segregation. Sometimes it can be done with select words or phrases.

In 1988, Jesse Jackson popularized the term *African American*[12] by suggesting black people born in this country should adopt this term as a way of celebrating their African ties and culture. Other ethnic groups, such as *German Americans* and *Irish Americans* had already adopted similar terms in order to celebrate their heritages. At the time, much of the white community saw the term *African American* as no more than yet another example of PC-based sensitivities. Other whites saw it as another example of self-segregation.

The morning after Martin Luther King Jr. was assassinated, a teacher in Riceville, Iowa, taught her third-grade class a valuable lesson about discrimination and segregation. Jane Elliott divided her students into two groups: *blue-eyed* people and *brown-eyed* people.[13] She had the brown-eyed students wear collars so they could be easily identified from a distance. She explained to children that blue-eyed people were superior to brown-eyed people. She told them blue-eyed people were smarter, cleaner, and better behaved than brown-eyed people.

Because of their *inferiority*, the brown-eyed children were given a number of restrictions on their daily activities. They were told not to play with the blue-eyed children, nor were they allowed to use playground equipment. They were also instructed not to drink directly from the water fountains; they were to use a paper cup instead. The brown-eyed children had to wait for the blue-eyed children to go to lunch before them, and when it was their turn, they were not allowed to go back for seconds.

Because Elliott was their teacher—a person they saw as an authority figure—they complied with her instructions and quickly fell into their respective roles. In the course of one school day, the class was transformed from a civil, cooperative group of students into a segregated, socially distinctive society.

Many of the blue-eyed children relished in their perceived superior status. When asked later how being superior to brown-eyed people made them feel, some blue-eyed students would speak of enjoying the sense of power they had over their classmates. In a lesson taught two years later to another class, one of the boys mentioned how it made him "feel like a king."

The brown-eyed children became shocked at how they were now being treated by children who had been their close friends just the day before. They almost instantly began suffering from low self-esteem and became angry and resentful.

The next day, Elliott reversed the roles. She told the class she had lied the day before, and it was the brown-eyed people who were superior over the blue-eyed people. She had the brown-eyed students place their collars on the blue-eyed students and ordered the same restrictions on the blue-eyed students she had previously imposed on the brown-eyed ones. The results were the same.

After the second day, Elliott explained to her class what she had done and why she had done it. As you might imagine, the children were relieved to find out they were no longer different and quickly renewed their friendships. Some may see what Jane Elliott did to her students as cruel, but it did teach them a lifelong lesson about not judging people for how they look.

In 1970, William Peters filmed Elliott teaching this lesson to another class in a documentary for ABC news called *The Eye of the Storm*.[14] In 1985, Peters produced another documentary for PBS/Frontline called *A Class Divided*.[15] In the second film, Peters showed footage from *The Eye of the Storm* as well as a mini-reunion of some of the students from that film.

The former third-grade students spoke of the lessons they had learned that week about discrimination and how many of them had passed those lessons on to their children. They also repeatedly spoke of how that experience had left them with a sense of being family with their former classmates. Perhaps that is a lesson we all should learn.

In the case of the MBA and the term African American, I believe the original intent was that of an overall positive nature. The problem with self-segregation is, no matter what its original intent, and regardless of which group decides to endorse this practice, it becomes a double-edged sword. While it may be an effective tool in the fight to end oppression and instill cultural pride, over time, it's more likely to tear people apart rather than establish unity.

Unlike the short-term case of the third-grade class in Iowa, in the long term, it is difficult for most people to accept the concept, which states, "In order for us to finally come together, we must again go our separate ways." If the road to unity is paved with self-segregation, it quickly becomes a one-way, dead-end street.

It is no coincidence I began this chapter with a quote by Martin Luther King Jr. In his famous "I Have a Dream" speech, Dr. King said,[16]

I have a dream that my four little children will one day live in a nation where they will not be judged by the color of their skin, but by the content of their character.

He ended his speech with these immortal words, which I believe should be remembered by all:

When we let freedom to ring, when we let it ring from every village and every hamlet, from every state and every city, we will be able to speed up that day when all of God's children, black men and white men, Jews and Gentiles, Protestants and Catholics, will be able to join hands and sing in the words of the old Negro spiritual, "Free at last! Free at last! Thank God Almighty, we are free at last!"

With racism, the practice of political correctness has created an atmosphere that causes many to make extremely negative assumptions when any opinions involving the causes of racial differences are openly expressed by the majority. Due to the increased sensitivities political correctness has created regarding ethnic groups, this is especially true during discussion of possible mistakes made by minorities. Put another way, if fifty black men gather to discuss the causes of and find solutions to the problems involving racial differences, it is hailed as progressive continuation of the work done by the civil rights movement. When fifty white men gather for the same purpose, it is seen as a Klan meeting.

As long as we continue to allow PC to prevent us from the mere mention of a problem we all know exists, we will never be allowed to properly identify the problem and, therefore, never find a workable solution. If we cannot find a way to come together and put an end to racism, I fear Dr. King's dream will never be realized.

Chapter Five

Your Tax Dollars
At Work

Let the people think they govern and they will be governed.

—William Penn

To better understand the effect PC has on the masses, we must look at how it has historically been used by governments around the world. After all, it is called *political* correctness for a reason. By doing this, it will become more obvious that PC is not merely a less offensive form of everyday communication; instead, it is a very effective form of mind control.

It is commonly believed the terms *politically correct* and *political correctness* originated during the late 1970s or early 1980s. But the earliest citation of the term in the United States was found in the U.S. Supreme Court decision involving *Chisholm v. Georgia*[17] in 1793.

Alexander Chisholm, the executor of the estate of Robert Farquhar, attempted to sue the State of Georgia in the Supreme Court over payments due him for goods Farquhar had supplied Georgia during the American Revolutionary War. The State of Georgia refused to appear claiming that as a sovereign state, it is not legally required to appear in court to hear a suit against it that the State of Georgia did not consent to in the first place. The Supreme Court's decision was in favor of the plaintiff, noting the statement under judgment (whether or not Georgia should be required to appear in court) is literally incorrect. One of the justices wrote,

> *The states, rather than the People, for whose sakes the States exist, are frequently the objects which attract and arrest our principal attention . . . Sentiments and expressions of this inaccurate kind prevail in our common, even in our convivial, language. Is a toast asked? [To] "The United States," instead of [to] the "People of the United States," is the toast given. This is not politically correct.*

Simply put, the government exists to serve the people, not the other way around. We should not require the permission of any government to take legal action against it when we feel we have been treated unfairly by them.

Since that time, however, political correctness has been used as a way of controlling the hearts and minds of the people in order to trick them into thinking in ways they otherwise would not.

In her essay entitled, "Cultural Sensitivity and Political Correctness: The Linguistic Problem of Naming," Edna Andrews, a linguistics professor at Duke University, says that using inclusive and neutral language is based upon the idea that language represents, and may even control thought.[18] This essay suggests the reasonable deduction of cultural change via linguistic change. In other words, if a speaker changes the way he/she speaks, it could change the way the listener thinks.

Political correctness is generally thought of as a way of creating more sensitive or less offensive terminology in an effort to remove social stigmas and stereotypes. While it can be used as an effective tool to that end, it is more often used as a tool to further self-serving agendas.

When employed by governments, it is used in almost every form ranging from the sensitive approach to hard-core propaganda filled with tough negative rhetoric. Regardless of which form is used by politicians (or anyone else), their main objective remains the same: to use language designed to alter the thoughts of those they serve as well as the world.

A prime example of this was seen in Nazi Germany during the first half of the twentieth century. Adolf Hitler acquired popularity and power, in part, by appealing to the civic pride of what fellow Nazi, Alfred Rosenberg, called *Aryan-Nordic* people referring to them as the *master race*.

After gaining control of the Nazi Party and being appointed chancellor of Germany in January of 1933, Hitler began a fierce propaganda campaign against people he considered to be the enemies of Germany. Among these enemies were *non-Aryans*, homosexuals, and especially Jews. On April 11, 1933, Hitler's Nazis issued a decree defining a non-Aryan as[19]

anyone descended from non-Aryan, especially Jewish,
parents or grandparents. One parent or grandparent
classifies the descendant as non-Aryan . . . especially if
one parent or grandparent was of the Jewish faith.

Hitler believed the use of propaganda was vital in controlling the hearts and minds of the public. He first spoke of this theory in his 1926 book, *Mein Kampf*, where he said,[20]

Propaganda tries to force a doctrine upon an entire
people . . . Propaganda works on the community in the
sense of an idea and it makes it ripe for the time of the
victory of this idea.

To this end, he established the Reich Ministry of Public Enlightenment and Propaganda headed by Joseph Goebbels. Goebbels created an endless stream of negative propaganda against the Jews through all forms of media (radio, music, arts, the press, etc.)—so much so that in a very short time, the Jews were transformed from ordinary citizens to the most hated people in Germany.

Shortly after his rise to power, Hitler also opened a secret campaign of genocide against the Jews in Germany. This secret campaign was known by Nazi leaders as the final solution. He later expanded this campaign to include German-occupied countries during World War II. After the end of the war, when the full extent of the atrocities committed by the Nazis became known, the final solution became known as the Holocaust.

Whether it is used to restore civic pride in post-World War I Germany or mandated by a communist régime, PC is a form of propaganda used to control the masses.

Since its founding in 1949, the People's Republic of China has virtually eliminated freedom of speech by banning religions and allowing only Marxism and Maoism as the politically correct belief system. The practice of contradicting these state sanctioned theologies could lead (and often did) to prison sentences, death, or both. During the decade long Cultural Revolution (1966-1976), people took great care with their words to avoid any possible misinterpretation which could be seen as a contradiction of either Karl Marx or Mao Zedong. In Marxist-Leninist and Trotskyite vocabulary, the word *correct* was commonly used to describe the *appropriate party line* and therefore the ideologically *correct line*. In spite of protests that have occurred within China, most Chinese citizens dare not challenge the authority of official political doctrine.

I have no doubt some will consider the situation in China an extreme example of how a government using the tool of PC can and does control the hearts and minds of its people. Those who are of this opinion may also point out such things could never happen in this country because of our right to freedom of speech. I feel safe in assuming similar thoughts were in the minds of millions of Chinese before 1949.

But it is not only leaders of foreign nations who use PC.

During his two terms in office (1981-1989), Ronald Reagan dedicated much of his time to the destruction of communism and the downfall of the Soviet Union. In doing so, he also put an end to the four-decade-long Cold War between the two nations. To this end, Reagan began a campaign of tough rhetoric against the Soviets by calling them an evil empire whose leaders assumed the *right to commit any crime*. In 1981, he backed up his rhetoric by bolstering the military strength of the United States with a trillion dollar defense buildup. Both nations then targeted intermediate-range nuclear missiles at each other in Europe.

In 1983, Reagan applied further pressure on the Soviet leaders by proposing a plan to build a shield against intercontinental ballistic missiles involving space-based weapons. This plan, officially named the Strategic Defense Initiative, was later dubbed the *Star Wars* defense by the news media. It also removed the previous concept of *Mutual Assured Destruction* that assumed neither side would start a nuclear war because it would be unable to avoid imminent destruction by the other.

The basic strategy behind these actions was to force the Soviet Union to engage in a costly arms race it could not afford due to an already-troubled economy. Many analysts believe Reagan's plan succeeded in triggering further Soviet economic difficulties that played a major role in the eventual collapse of the Soviet Union in 1991.

The challenges faced by Reagan were enormous due to the economic and social state of the United States at the time. In 1981, the United States was engulfed in one of the worst recessions in its history. Due to the turbulent times of the sixties and seventies, the level of patriotism and national pride was at an all-time low. One of the best ways for any government to restore national pride in its people is to provide a cause. For his plan to have any chance of success, he began the tough rhetoric in order to gain public support in the United States for the massive expenditures his plan would incur.

Whether or not Reagan's actions were justifiable is a debate I shall leave for others. But, in my opinion, it is a good illustration of how *insensitive* terminology can also be used as PC. Referring to the Soviet Union as an evil empire greatly enhanced the already-negative perception most Americans had about their main adversary at the time. Part of the rhetoric was aimed at the human rights violations the Soviet government imposed on its own citizens. This caused many Americans to view the Soviets, not just as an adversary with nuclear capabilities but also as a global menace that had to be stopped—no matter what the costs.

Reagan was by no means the first president to use political correctness to further an agenda, or the last.

On June 25, 1950, North Korea (Democratic People's Republic of Korea) invaded South Korea (Republic of Korea) after Korean national-peninsular reunification talks stalled. President Harry S. Truman ordered Gen. Douglas MacArthur to transfer matériel to the Army of the Republic of Korea (South Korea) and provide air cover to the evacuation of U.S. nationals. After American and South Korean forces suffered severe casualties in the initial battles and were forced to retreat south, Truman ordered in reinforcements thereby plunging the United States deep into the Korean War.

Since the American public was still battle weary from World War II, which had just ended only a few years before, Congress was reluctant to issue a formal declaration of war against North Korea. In an effort to justify his actions, Truman referred to the Korean conflict as a *police action,* which was *pertinent to the American global containment of communism.*

Truman believed the United States was obligated to repel the invasion by North Korea, paralleling it with Adolf Hitler's aggressions in the 1930s. He also had concerns about repeating the mistake of appeasement made by the United States and others in regard to Hitler's early actions. These thoughts were reflected in a statement in which he said,[21]

> *Communism was acting in Korea, just as Hitler, Mussolini and the Japanese had ten, fifteen, and twenty years earlier. I felt certain that if South Korea was allowed to fall Communist leaders would be emboldened to override nations closer to our own shores. If the Communists were permitted to force their way into the Republic of Korea without opposition from the free world, no small nation would have the courage to resist threat and aggression by stronger Communist neighbors.*

Similar reasoning led to the U.S. involvement in the Vietnam War. Although on August 7, 1964, Congress passed the so-called Tonkin Gulf Resolution, which gave President Lyndon B. Johnson the authority to use military force in Southeast Asia as he saw fit, no formal declaration of war was ever declared. For this reason, many people in the government, as well as members of the press, would also occasionally refer to the war as a police action.

American military involvement (advisors and combat troops) in the Vietnam War lasted almost two decades, making it the longest war in American history. The human cost of the war was tremendous. There were estimated death tolls of 3 to 4 million Vietnamese from both sides, and 1.5 to 2 million Laotians and Cambodians. United States casualty figures include over 58,000 killed, over 303,000 wounded, and over 1,700 still missing in action to this day.[22]

The combined casualty figures—killed, wounded, and missing—from all nations involved in the Korean War totaled nearly three million military personnel and countless numbers of civilians;

and these figures do not include the millions of family members and friends who were deeply affected by the fate of their loved ones. With the amount of bloodshed and human suffering that occurred around the world because of the wars in Korea and Vietnam, I believe the term *police action* falls horribly short.

In this vein, I wish to digress for a moment from the overall subject matter of political correctness to say something, which I believe to be very long overdue.

I have the utmost respect for the men and women who serve (past, present, and future) in the military of this country in times of peace and in times of war. I believe their dedication and the sacrifices they have made and continue to make for our nation, to be both admirable and honorable.

Although the following statements should in *no* way be perceived as diminishment or exclusion of the tremendous sacrifices made by the veterans of other American wars, I would like to send a special message to veterans of the Vietnam War.

As I said before, I spent my childhood in the turbulent times of the sixties and seventies—during the time of the Vietnam War. Because I had friends and relatives who were stationed in combat zones, I found myself glued to our television watching the evening news almost every night in hopes of catching a glimpse of a familiar face, but at the same time hoping the face I might recognize would not be one of those I saw on stretchers or in body bags. Fortunately, all the members of my family who served returned home safely—or so I thought. Unfortunately, others I knew did not.

For the first time in my young life, at around seven or eight years old, I began to realize the horrors of and the reality of war. This was not some old war movie I had seen on the *Late Late Show*. There were no actors on the screen. These were real people being shot at with real bullets and spilling real blood. I sat in horror as I watched soldiers engaging in fierce combat. I soon realized these people were not only fighting for their country but also for their very lives. To this day, I can only imagine the thoughts going through their minds.

It was on these same news programs I witnessed something that left me just as horrified. I saw scenes of soldiers coming home who had survived the war being spit on by war protesters. In some cases, these misguided protesters would throw blood on the soldiers, and in both cases would call them such things as "baby killers." During that time, I heard reports that some of the more radical protesters would send anonymous letters to the parents of soldiers killed in action telling them how happy they were that their son had been killed while murdering the *noble communist freedom fighters* from North Vietnam. At first, I had a hard time believing that someone could be as sick and twisted to write something like that to grieving parents even if they did feel that way. That changed when I was shown a letter sent to one of those parents—another hard life lesson learned.

I have always respected the right of anyone to protest—a right that is granted and protected by the Constitution. However, I found it highly hypocritical for these protesters to attack the people who risked their lives to protect the protesters' right to protest. And I still do. If you wish to blame someone for the atrocities of war, blame the politicians—on both sides—whose lack of responsibility creates wars in the first place.

According to the U.S. military code of conduct, while each soldier is held accountable for their own actions, their commanders are ultimately responsible for the overall actions of the soldiers under their command. Since the president of the United States is also our military commander in chief, it stands to reason that this would be the best place to start. The same could be said about the leaders of all nations.

As the soldiers began to return home from the war, I began to realize, even if they had no physical wounds, most, if not all, had psychological wounds. Due to the incredible horrors they witnessed and experienced, some of these soldiers found it impossible to separate the realities of their time spent in combat and life back in—as they often called it—the real world. They found themselves mentally trapped in the jungles and rice paddies of Southeast Asia. Through the passage of time, and often through counseling, some have found their way back while others still remain. With all this in mind, to all the veterans of the Vietnam War, here is my—and other like-minded American's—message:

Regardless of whether or not this was a so-called just war, there are no mere words that can even begin to accurately describe the level of appreciation I have for those of you who made so many sacrifices, both at home and abroad, by serving your country during the Vietnam War. Although these words fall incredibly short, I wish to say thank-you for your service. And to those of you who found yourselves trapped but managed to find your way back, I say welcome home, you were missed. And to those who still find themselves fighting, I say it's time to come home; we miss you and we are waiting for you.

As I sit here looking over what I just wrote, I realize that I have not digressed at all. In fact, this is a perfect example of the huge influence PC can have on the thoughts and actions of an entire society.

As I said before, I have no ill feelings toward average American citizens who felt the war in Vietnam was a travesty and wanted it to end. I do, however, hold malice toward the radical factions who committed what I believe to be crimes against our soldiers and the people of this country far beyond simple assault.

These radical protesters embedded themselves inside a group of people known as hippies who felt a desire to see changes made in the way governments and society itself operated. Most of the hippies were young and idealistic with no real organized direction in which to advance their movement. This made them easy targets for the propaganda of radical protesters' agendas. They taught hippies to fight against the *establishment* by wearing the symbols of peace and by chanting the "make love, not war!" types of slogans I previously mentioned.

To end the U.S. military involvement in Vietnam, they ironically and hypocritically used a tactic straight out of the military handbook: divide and conquer. The goal of these groups was to divide public opinion through radical means and remove support for our troops. Without that support, the main focus would then shift to the war itself. To that end, the radical protesters were successful.

Even though we as Americans have not always agreed with the reasons our leaders have given us for going to war, once at war, we have always shown tremendous support for those who fought in them. By spitting, throwing blood, and calling the soldiers baby killers, the radical protesters drew a great deal of media attention to themselves and their cause. At that time in our history, these actions caused many to question what, if any, atrocities were being committed by our soldiers.

Although most Americans still supported our soldiers privately, it became politically incorrect to show that support openly. There were very few parades thrown for troops returning from Vietnam—parades that were so prevalent in previous wars.

During and after World War II, any person in a military uniform would usually be greeted with smiles, a pat on the back, and often asked by the greeter if there was anything they could do for the soldier. In the case of the Vietnam veterans, this was rarely seen.

Many of the leaders of the radical protesters were professors employed by our colleges and universities. These professors used their positions to convince students and others to fight the establishment by using various forms of protest. These protests ranged from so-called sit-ins to young men publicly burning their draft notices and moving to Canada to avoid being arrested for refusing to serve.

While the people protested, many of these professors wrote articles and/or books about the war, its causes, and who profited from it the most. By doing so, previously unknown scholars could obtain almost overnight notoriety and fame. This could also provide them with job security, large fees for speaking tours, and the means by which to promote the sale of their books.

The perception that these individuals were intelligent professionals gave apparent credibility to their cause in the minds of the *freedom fighters* they controlled. If you asked me, I would say this was nothing more than another case of a group of self-centered individuals who convinced average people to do their dirty work for them in an effort to further their own agendas. It was hypocrisy at its worst.

To justify their actions and the actions of their followers, these leaders praised their efforts as the work of *intellectual, progressively thinking, and open-minded people*. If I had been given the chance to speak to the activists regarding their treatment of our troops, I would have suggested they consider another point of view before marching onto the battlefield to carry out their plans inspired by people who had indoctrinated them. While being open-minded is a beautiful thing, beware of becoming so open-minded your brain falls out.

According to some psychologists, the lack of public support upon their return was a major contributing factor to the mental anguish many Vietnam veterans suffered and suffer still. It is for this and many other reasons I consider the actions of those radical protesters to be criminal. I have never been an advocate of suing people at the drop of a hat. However, I would find it very difficult to blame any Vietnam veteran who suffered or still suffers such mental anguish for seeking legal counsel.

It is most unfortunate that there are people in this world who take advantage of the suffering or passions of others for personal gain. They usually obtain their goals of wealth and power without regard to the price paid by those they manipulate. I have found this to be true whether it is done by individuals or by governments.

Throughout the history of the United States, there have been pivotal moments that have led this country into war. Always preceding those pivotal moments were political failures that created tensions, which inevitably led to military action. The following are a few examples of those military actions: *the shot heard around the world* at Concord, Massachusetts (April 19, 1775), which started the Revolutionary War; the attack on Fort Sumter (April 12-13, 1861), which began the American Civil War; the Japanese attack on Pearl Harbor (December 7, 1941), which plunged the United States into World War II; and the terrorist attacks on the World Trade Center in New York City, the Pentagon in Washington DC as well as the downed plane in Pennsylvania (September 11, 2001, commonly referred to as 9/11), which led to the so-called Global War on Terror (GWOT) also known as War on Terror or Long War.

On September 20, 2001, then president George W. Bush addressed a joint session of Congress and announced his intentions to eliminate terrorist groups around the world, thereby beginning the GWOT by saying,[23]

Our war on terror begins with al Qaeda, but it does not end there. It will not end until every terrorist group of global reach has been found, stopped and defeated.

Shortly afterward, because of public outrage over 9/11 and in an apparent desire to aid President Bush, Congress quickly approved a bill known as the USA Patriot Act of 2001, which is an acronym for *Uniting and Strengthening America by Providing Appropriate Tools Required to Intercept and Obstruct Terrorism Act of 2001*. President Bush signed the bill into law on October 26, 2001, just forty-five days after the attacks.

Critics of this bill claim many of its components violate civil liberties of people in the United States thus making those components (if not the entire law) unconstitutional. After reading the wording of the actual law, I agree. The USA Patriot Act undermines basic rights granted by the Constitution to people living inside the United States. It virtually gives law enforcement agencies such as the FBI an almost free hand to investigate whomever they wish and for whatever reason they choose, all without first showing just cause to obtain a warrant from the court.

Provisions of the USA Patriot Act[24] allow the FBI and other agencies to investigate which books a person checks out of a library, what websites they visit, their e-mail communications, etc. The investigating agency's only requirement to conduct such searches is to merely state that the subject of the court order is part of an "authorized investigation" and to insure that "such investigation of a United States person is not conducted solely upon the basis of activities protected by the first amendment to the Constitution" (SEC. 214. (a)(1)).

It is far too easy to falsely claim someone is part of an authorized investigation not solely based on the exercise of their first amendment rights. It is yet another to provide proof that investigation is legitimate through the standards set by the Fourth amendment—the *probable cause* clause. Allowing a one-size-fits-all provision leaves the door too wide open for abuse.

Ironically, engaging in activities protected by the First Amendment of the Constitution can often cause a person to become a suspect in international or domestic terrorism. Let's take a look at a hypothetical situation to illustrate.

Fred Johnson goes with friends to a restaurant, has a few drinks, and engages in a conversation about current events. He begins expressing his dislike of the way the government is handling the war in Iraq and suggests a change in leadership is in order. Fred is overheard by a person at a nearby table who doesn't like him or disagrees with his views. The second person takes notes of what Fred says and reports him to the local office of the FBI the next day. The FBI, in spite of the fact the investigation doesn't uncover much evidence pointing to his being a terrorist, places him on the terrorist watch list as a precaution.

Because he is now on the terrorist watch list, Fred, who travels frequently on business, is detained for hours every time he attempts to board an airplane. During his detention, he is not given an explanation as to why he is being detained. He is also not read his rights, allowed to leave, allowed to make a phone call to let his family know what is happening to him, nor is he allowed to have legal counsel present during questioning. Interrogators find nothing and eventually let him go but keep his name on the list.

A few months later, another FBI agent is listening to surveillance tapes of a suspected terrorist and hears the alleged terrorist mention that he has sought the assistance of a totally different man who, by coincidence, is also named Fred Johnson. The agent checks the database of the terrorist watch list and finds the original Fred Johnson listed and notifies his superiors. One thing leads to another and before you know it, there is a court order to investigate innocent Fred.

The FBI goes to Fred's local library, hands the clerk a copy of the court order and demands to look at any and all records the library has on Fred. They then go to his Internet provider and do the same thing. They check Fred's e-mails, what websites he visits, and any other information which may be obtained. Next the FBI breaks into Fred's home, copies the contents of his computer's hard drive, rummages through his belongings, and plants electronic listening devices. They can do all this totally without Fred's knowledge, and because of the Patriot Act, they can also do it legally.

The USA Patriot Act allows for delaying notification of a warrant to a suspect indefinitely. There are also sections of this law that make it illegal (as in Fred's case) for the librarian or the Internet provider to inform Fred the FBI ever looked at his records let alone what they found.

Since the company Fred works for deals exclusively with sensitive government contracts, Fred's security clearance gets revoked. Without any other projects to work on, Fred's employer has no choice but to let him go. Because of this, other companies with work in his field will not hire him, and he is forced to find work in areas that pay much lower salaries. All this happened because he dared to exercise his constitutionally protected right of free speech.

If you think this is an unlikely scenario, or this could not happen to you, I suggest doing a little research. You may be surprised at what you find. The American Civil Liberties Union's website lists some improbable people who were, or are still, on the watch list. Below are a few of the names they listed:[25]

> *Robert Johnson*—60 Minutes *interviewed 12 men named Robert Johnson, all of whom reported being pulled aside and interrogated, sometimes for hours, nearly every time they go to the airport.*

> *Marine Staff Sgt. Daniel Brown was blocked from flying while on his way home from an 8-month deployment in Iraq. He was listed as a suspected terrorist due to a previous incident in which gunpowder was detected on his boots, most likely residue from a previous tour in Iraq.*

> *James Moore, author of a book critical of the Bush Administration called* Bush's Brain.

> *Congresswoman Loretta Sanchez (D-CA) has reportedly had problems flying.*

U.S. Senator Edward Kennedy (D, Mass.) After repeated delays at airport security, the senator had trouble getting removed from the airline watch list despite calls to Homeland Security and eventually a personal conversation with the Secretary of DHS.

9/11 Hijackers. While certainly these were individuals we all wish had been watched out for, they are, in fact, dead. Yet, the names of 14 of the 19 hijackers from 9/11 were on a copy of the list obtained by 60 Minutes. More evidence the list is poorly maintained and full of junk names which will only serve to ensnare the innocent.

Nelson Mandela, winner of the Nobel Peace Prize and a household name all over the world, is listed on the U.S. watch list and needs special permission to enter the United States.

John William Anderson, age 6. Among those caught up by the no-fly list are many infants and small children.

The USA Patriot Act is the result of a brutal attack by terrorists, public outrage over those attacks, public fear that more attacks are imminent, and the hasty reaction of Congress and the Bush administration to settle those fears.

I have found most politicians to be like flags; they fly in the direction of the prevailing wind. There was so much pressure on Congress to pass this legislation that very few members of Congress bothered to read the entire bill before voting. For this, and other reasons, I believe most members of Congress felt such urgency to pass this bill because they believed it was literally politically correct to do so.

It is no coincidence this law is named the USA Patriot Act. In order to maintain public support for the law, some government officials, and even some members of the press, publically criticized those who questioned the constitutionality of the law. They dubbed these people nonpatriots or unpatriotic, again, for exercising their right of free speech and free press. Some even suggested those *nonpatriots* are guilty of treason.

We as a people, and as a government of the people, have made a multitude of mistakes since the first shots fired at Concord. It bears repeating: the worst offense a patriot can commit against their country is to do nothing. I believe every citizen in this country has not only the right to speak out against what they believe to be wrong in this nation but also the patriotic duty to do so. Having the freedom to exchange ideas and viewpoints "in order to form a more perfect union" is exactly what our founding fathers had in mind. It is the very essence of what the concept of freedom of speech is all about. Any attempt to undermine or remove such freedoms comes much closer to treason than exercising them ever will.

In the early months of Barrack Obama's term as president, I noticed a totally opposite approach to the GWOT and terrorists in general. But that change, at first, had only seemed to be in the terminology used to describe them.

On March 25, 2009, major news agencies reported that a memo was allegedly sent via e-mail from the Office of Management and Budget to Pentagon staff members, which advised,[26]

> *This administration prefers to avoid using the term "Long War" or "Global War on Terror" [GWOT.] Please use "Overseas Contingency Operation."*

It further went on to advise Pentagon personnel to "please pass this on to your speechwriters and try to catch this change before statements make it to OMB."

The Office of Management and Budget is the executive-branch agency, which reviews the public testimony of administration officials before it is delivered. Kenneth Baer (an OMB spokesman) later told reporters:

> *There was no memo, no guidance . . . This is the opinion of a career civil servant.*

At this point, I am a bit confused as to how an *opinion of a career civil servant* could have possibly shown up in a memo that didn't exist in the first place, but I digress.

Although many administration officials have denied the existence of this memo and the guidance it suggests, the term *overseas contingency operations* has been widely used by several members of Obama's administration.

When discussing Obama's budget proposal at a news conference on February 26, 2009, OMB director Peter Orszag said,

> *The budget shows the combined cost of operations in Iraq, Afghanistan and any other overseas contingency operations that may be necessary.*

In congressional testimony given in March 2009, Craig W. Duehring, assistant secretary of the air force for manpower, said,

> *Key battlefield monetary incentives has allowed the Air Force to meet the demands of overseas contingency operations even as requirements continue to grow.*

A Pentagon spokesman reportedly said there was no memo or specific directive instructing officials to stop using the GWOT phrase but acknowledged that the department has officially adopted *overseas contingency operation* as the new term for the wars in Iraq and Afghanistan.

When U.S. secretary of state Hillary Clinton was asked about the new term, she said,

> *The administration has stopped using the phrase and I think that speaks for itself. I haven't heard it used. I haven't gotten any directive about using it or not using it, it's just not being used.*

Since no one person could possibly handle the enormous job of running every department of government simultaneously, administration officials—department heads and others—are in place to assist the president in his or her day-to-day duties of running the federal government. In doing so, they are expected to conduct business in such a manner that accurately reflects the policies and directives of the President.

That said, and given the fact so many people in Obama's administration had switched from using GWOT to Overseas Contingency Operation (all at about the same time), I find it difficult to believe this policy shift did not come from some form of directive from the President, even if it was only verbally. Are we to believe that it is merely a coincidence so many people began using this term without a directive? Or that they would be allowed to continue its use without executive approval? And why are officials within the administration trying so hard to deny a directive exists? I have to agree with Secretary Clinton—that does speak for itself.

I believed President Obama chose this change in terminology to distance his administration from the rhetoric of the Bush administration and to appease allies in Europe who felt usage of the GWOT term was counterproductive and did not accurately describe the wars.

On the latter, I could not disagree more. I think when people are being attacked on a daily basis because of military operations, it is called war. When soldiers are wounded or killed because of military conflict, it is called war. When the buildings and infrastructures of nations are being destroyed because of military battles taking place within their borders, it is called war. And when a group or groups of radical political and/or religious extremists (terrorists) crash planes into the towers of the World Trade Center, the Pentagon, and a field in Pennsylvania killing over three thousand innocent people, it is most definitely called war. Have we forgotten the lessons of Pearl Harbor?

Even *terrorism* is another word that has been changed by the Obama administration. In her first testimony to Congress as homeland security secretary, Janet Napolitano referred to terrorism as man-caused disasters. Secretary Napolitano explained her reasoning behind this terminology to the German news agency Spiegel by saying,[27]

> That is perhaps only a nuance, but it demonstrates that we want to move away from the politics of fear toward a policy of being prepared for all risks that can occur.

Speaking of politics of fear, while the Obama administration was working so hard to tone down what they say in public, apparently those rules didn't apply to private communications. But even some of those communications illustrate an apparent desire to manipulate public opinion.

On April 7, 2009, an assessment report prepared by the Extremism and Radicalization Branch, Homeland Environment Threat Analysis Division, DHS apparently warns law enforcement agencies to keep an eye on returning veterans from the wars in Iraq and Afghanistan because they may join right-wing extremist groups such as the white supremacists.[28] Although this has taken place on very rare occasions, such as in the case of Timothy McViegh[29], I really doubt it is a common problem with our servicemen and women. The *scope* section of this assessment report reads,

> This product is one of a series of intelligence assessments published by the Extremism and Radicalization Branch to facilitate a greater understanding of the phenomenon of violent radicalization in the United States. The information is provided to federal, state, local, and tribal counterterrorism and law enforcement officials so they may effectively deter, prevent, preempt, or respond to terrorist attacks against the United States. Federal efforts to influence domestic public opinion must be conducted in an overt and transparent manner, clearly identifying United States Government sponsorship.

Secretary Napolitano seems to prefer calling attacks committed by terrorists who murder thousands of Americans *man-caused disasters*, but apparently has no problem calling those who fight terrorists in the battlefield potential extremists. That sounds to me like a huge pile of PC crap. It also sounds like a convenient excuse to place returning veterans who speak out about what really went on over there on a terrorist watch list.

And here is a thought: if there really is a potential problem with our troops (or anything else for that matter), how about informing the public in an honest manner and letting us decide instead of going along with "federal efforts to influence domestic public opinion." Influencing domestic public opinion is nothing short of federal propaganda for the purpose of mind control.

Evidently the information in the DHS assessment report was not meant for the general public to read in the first place. At the bottom of the same page is the following disclaimer:

> **Warning:** This document is UNCLASSIFIED//FOR OFFICIAL USE ONLY (U//FOUO). It contains information that may be exempt from public release under the Freedom of Information Act (5 U.S.C. 552). It is to be controlled, stored, handled, transmitted, distributed, and disposed of in accordance with DHS policy relating to FOUO information and is not to be released to the public, the media, or other personnel who do not have a valid need-to-know without prior approval of an authorized DHS official. State and local homeland security officials may share this document with authorized security personnel without further approval from DHS.

It appears as though someone inside DHS thought the American people needed to know. I have no idea who that person is, but I would love to buy him or her a drink some day.

What part of the words *war* and *terrorism* do these politicians *not* understand?

I do not intend the upcoming statement to be seen in any way as an attempt to make light of the tragic events of 9/11. In fact, my wish is to demonstrate just how ridiculous and seemingly uncaring the use of specially selected PC words or phrases can be.

I suspect that if the Obama administration had been in office during the attacks of 9/11, their official press release would have sounded something like this:

> This morning, in New York City, the twin towers of the World Trade Center suffered a "loss of structural integrity" due to a rapidly expanding chemical reaction creating a man-caused disaster. A similar man-caused disaster has created a partial loss of structural integrity to a government building in Washington, D.C. In a third occurrence, a commercial airline has failed to maintain flight status over Pennsylvania. Preliminary reports say there are over three thousand persons who have suffered permanent loss of all vital organ functions due to these events. President Obama is, at this time, meeting with advisors to discuss possible overseas contingency operations in response to these occurrences.

By referring to terrorism as man-caused disasters and wars as overseas contingency operations simply to distance their rhetoric from that of their predecessors, the Obama administration has shown a blatant disregard for the pain and suffering of the people most affected by terrorist attacks. I would not want to be the person who has the duty of informing someone's parents their son or daughter was killed because of a *man-caused disaster*, or in an *overseas contingency operation*. If it were my child, I would want to be told the truth, no matter how ugly that truth may be.

While I respect the rights of those in government to voice their opinions, I believe it is the responsibility of public officials to be honest with the American people. We are not children who need to be sheltered or bombarded with phrases that make very bad situations seem less than they are. It is always best to deal with issues by fully disclosing the true facts associated with them, no matter what those facts may be.

As far as the members of the press are concerned, unless you clearly indicate that the statements you are about to make are nothing more than an editorial opinion, stick to the honest facts and let the public make up their own minds. Don't leave out certain details to make the politician(s) who share your personal or professional agendas look good; it's called lying to the people, and we will eventually discover the truth.

And finally, to my readers, I would strongly suggest not believing the first thing you see, hear, or read. Do your own research, get news information from multiple sources, evaluate all the evidence, consider all points of view from as many different perspectives as possible, and most importantly, think for yourselves. If you take this advice, whatever conclusion you come to in the end will be your own and not one that has been instilled by those who want to brainwash you. It is risky and dangerous to blindly follow others as they often have their own agendas. It is important to remember, those with their own agendas rarely, if ever, have your best interests at heart.

CHAPTER SIX

Making Headlines

Most of the change we think we see in life is due to truths being in and out of favor.

—Robert Frost

There is little doubt the lawmaking process in the United States is reactionary. The next time you hear about a tragic event on the news, see how long it takes lawmakers to introduce a bill to prevent this event from ever happening again. In too many cases, not only do these new pieces of legislation fail to prevent another occurrence, but they also often add to the problem by creating a series of unnecessary regulations, excessive penalties, and the potential for frivolous lawsuits. They also cause something vital to the success of our nation and the world to be added to the endangered species list: common sense.

Lawmakers love the opportunity to be seen by the public as champions of a cause. It gives them plenty of exposure through media coverage—exposure that provides them with face and name recognition with voters so important to them during their reelection campaigns. Often, these politicians will choose a sensitive PC issue to make a stand. In some cases, they choose to introduce redundant legislation under new names. An example of this is legislation already in place and bills currently under consideration involving so-called hate crimes.

According to section 280003(a) of the Violent Crime Control and Law Enforcement Act of 1994, a hate crime is defined as[30]

> *(a) DEFINITION—In this section, "hate crime" means a crime in which the defendant intentionally selects a victim, or in the case of a property crime, the property that is the object of the crime, because of the actual or perceived race, color, religion, national origin, ethnicity, gender, disability, or sexual orientation of any person.*

Bills currently before Congress wish to extend this coverage to include gender identity and the homeless.

Supporters of such legislation suggest that hate crimes should be considered in a separate class of crime just like the different degrees of murder. While I agree that hate crimes are rightfully considered socially different, I also believe there are sufficient laws on the books to properly handle these cases without the need for special legislation. Simply put, assault is assault, arson is arson, and murder is murder. The reasons why people commit these crimes is called motive.

I also believe such legislation provides far too much opportunity for abuse and manipulation of our legal system for personal and political gain. To explain my point, I will use two versions of a hypothetical scenario.

A white man and a Jewish man are in a bar having a drink. The Jewish man accidently spills his drink on the white man. Even though the Jewish man apologizes for the accident, the white man punches him in the face. The white man is restrained by fellow patrons, the police are called, and the white man is charged with simple assault. In court, the white man pleads guilty, is placed on probation, pays a fine, and probably never overreacts in a similar situation again.

In the second version of this scenario, the white man calls the Jewish man a racially derogatory name in the heat of the moment. The police are called and the white man is charged with simple assault. The Jewish man is insulted by the assault mixed with a racial slur. He hires a lawyer who obtains the support of a high profile politician who has been a major supporter of hate crime legislation. The politician immediately calls a press conference, where he publically denounces the assault as an "obvious racially and religiously motivated hate crime" and demands that "social justice be served not only for the man who was attacked but for the entire Jewish community."

Because of the increased political pressure placed upon him due to this press conference and subsequent media coverage, the district attorney decides to change the charge from simple assault to a hate crime. At the trial, the DA produces witnesses who have heard the defendant use racial slurs (although rarely) in the past. In his closing arguments, he claims the white man struck the Jewish man not because of a spilled drink but because of his anti-Semitic views.

Before they enter into deliberations, the judge instructs the jury to decide guilt or innocence based strictly on the letter of the law. That is to say, does this case follow the guidelines set forth by the current legislation against hate crimes? Although the jury believes this is a case blown way out of proportion, they have no choice but to find the white man guilty. The white man is then sentenced to five to ten years in prison.

Under the provisions of certain hate crime laws, had the jury found him not guilty, the federal government could have set aside the verdict and convicted him anyway. The provisions allow the federal government to reprosecute people accused of hate crimes if (among other reasons), "the verdict or sentence obtained pursuant to State charges left demonstratively unvindicated the federal interest in eradicating bias-motivated violence." By the way, isn't there a little thing in the Constitution often referred to as double jeopardy, which makes this practice illegal?

A week after the verdict, the attorney, on behalf of the Jewish man, files a suit in civil court against the white man for damages due to *pain and suffering* caused by the incident. At the same time, the U.S. Justice Department files additional charges against the white man for *violating the civil rights* of the Jewish man. All this over a spilled drink, a heat of the moment racial slur, and a black eye?

So who benefits from the second version of this scenario? The Jewish man gets whatever monetary judgment he can, his lawyer gets his fees, the DA gets a conviction, and the "champion of social justice" politician gets reelected. Meanwhile, due to the intense media coverage, tensions between the white and Jewish communities are at an all-time high. I think this would not be justice at all; instead, it would be a gross miscarriage of justice.

We must also keep in mind that social justice is in no way the same as equal justice. *Social justice*—as it is commonly perceived today—is a system by which certain groups of people are given special privileges and rights because they are seen as being oppressed. *Equal justice* is a system where every man, woman, and child is treated and judged *equally* under the law and by society itself.

If this story was reversed and the Jewish man had assaulted the white man, I can't imagine a scenario where the Jewish man would have ever been given such a harsh sentence, nor should he. It is because of the ramifications of the mind-set created by the politically correct term *social justice* that such double standards exist.

If it was wrong for white people to have special privileges over minorities in the past, it is equally wrong for minorities to be given those privileges today. We should have equal justice in this country and throughout the world. Equal justice is what men like Dr. King fought and died for. It would be a travesty to allow their deaths to become in vain.

Had it not been for hate crime legislation, the first scenario would have most likely ended in one of two ways. The two men would have never spoken to each other again, or the white man would have apologized for his actions and offered to buy the Jewish man a drink. Which of the two scenarios do you think would have best served the public interest?

It is a common misconception that most hate crimes are committed by organized racially or ethnically biased groups in America. I was surprised to learn such groups account for approximately five percent of all hate crimes committed in the United States. If the truth were known, I imagine we would learn that a large number are committed by normal, everyday people in similar situations to the one I just described.

I believe true hate crimes are some of the most senseless crimes committed, and they should be punished to the fullest extent of the law. But we already have sufficient laws on the books to properly handle these cases—that is, if we don't allow PC to get in the way.

Before hate crime laws, several people were convicted of murders that were racially motivated. Some of these people were sentenced to death and executed. If they had been executed under a hate crime law, would that have made them more dead than those executed under the earlier laws? By creating special laws to deal with hate crimes, we are opening the door to more abuses of our legal system, which is already overworked. And if the wording of these laws allows criminals to walk free because of an inadvertently added loophole, have we really done such a great thing? Perhaps, instead of creating such redundant and useless legislation, our lawmakers should adopt the KISS method: Keep It Simple, Stupid.

If the current maximum penalties are insufficient to deal with lesser crimes such as assaults which are racially motivated, then change the current law to allow for higher penalties in those cases rather than creating new laws all together. This way, each case could be prosecuted on the merits of the of the case instead of a defendant such as the one I described above being preconvicted in the court of public opinion before the first witness is even called. If a conviction is warranted and obtained, it would allow the prosecutor and judge the freedom to ensure the punishment fits the crime without the prejudicial pressure from politically correct influences. In other words, they could use some common sense.

The above story was hypothetical. The following are some actual stories in the news from around the world that I believe show how society has lost a great deal of common sense because of PC.

For eighteen months, residents of Chandler, Arizona, were terrorized by a serial rapist, who came to be known as the Chandler Rapist. With very few leads, the Chandler Police Department had been working around the clock to identify and arrest the man responsible. As most police departments do in such situations, the Chandler police released a statement asking for help from the public. They published a sketch artist's rendition along with a brief general description of what the suspect looked like. The description the police gave was obtained from some of the twelve to fourteen-year-old girls who were the victims of the rapist. They described him as Hispanic, twenty-eight to forty years old, short with a muscular build, dark hair, and hazel or brown eyes.

A Spanish-speaking Phoenix news talk radio station complained to the police department about the description, claiming that *Hispanic* refers to an ethnicity, not a race. Mayra Nieves, vice president of programming reportedly said,[31]

> *Hispanic could be white, it could be black, it could be dark-skinned complexion. We Hispanics see it that way. I think this is racial profiling.*

Instead of referring to him as Hispanic, she said she would describe the Chandler Rapist as having "dark skin." My problem is deciding how to respond to just how ridiculous those statements are, but I will try.

In the first place, if the suspect had been a *white* Hispanic, I am fairly confident the victims would have described him as white. If he had been a *black* Hispanic, he would have been described as black.

Secondly, if the police are told, by the *victim*, a twelve-year-old girl, that a Hispanic man raped her, it is not racial profiling for the police to actually look for a man who fits that description. If the police then pass this description on to the public, it is not racial profiling. Instead, it is called good police work and common sense.

And third, if the police had used Mayra Nieves's description of having dark skin, then the public would have been looking out not only for Hispanic men but also black men, Arabic men, and every other race normally thought of as having dark skin complexions.

In a display of good police work and common sense, the Chandler Police Department refused to give in to the pressures of PC. Chandler police spokesman, Sgt. Rick Griner, said his department would stand by its description, and that they release the details the victims give them. "It would be irresponsible on our part to change or alter that," he said.

A suspect was finally arrested, with the assistance of a tip given to the police by a private citizen who (I might add) knew what to look for. The man charged with the crimes is Santana Batiz-Aceves, thirty-nine, a twice-deported illegal alien, and a Mexican national with a history of drug charges. Batiz-Aceves's DNA was later positively matched to that found at the crime scenes. He was booked on suspicion of twenty-five felonies including kidnapping, child molestation, sexual abuse, sexual conduct with a minor, aggravated assault, burglary, and trespassing. With this in mind, I say to Sgt. Rick Griner and the entire Chandler Police Department on their refusal to give in to PC, "Great call!"

This next story, which also takes place in Arizona, is an excellent example how some people wish to win support for their agendas by creating misleading terminology. They use PC terms that are designed to appeal to sensitivities leaving the reader or listener with a sense of obligation to support their causes. They also attempt to promote censorship by encouraging people in influential positions to ban the words used by those who oppose their views. When done properly, this tactic can be a very effective tool (albeit a highly unethical one) for achieving the goals of one's own agenda.

Los Abogados, the Hispanic Bar Association of Arizona, sent a letter to Ruth V. McGregor, the chief justice of the Supreme Court of Arizona, requesting her assistance in "disseminating some important information to Arizona's judges and their staff." The following is the message they requested Chief Justice McGregor to relay:[32]

> Specifically, we ask that you strongly encourage Arizona's judges and court employees to avoid using certain inflammatory immigrant-related terms in court documents, correspondence, and proceedings. Rather than describing the act that may have been committed by that person, these terms attach an illegal status to the person, thereby establishing a brand of contemptibility.

If I properly understand what Los Abogados is saying, they believe it is wrong to attach an illegal status to an illegal alien. To further explain what the authors of this letter were referring to, they wrote,

> Specifically, we highly discouraged use of the words "illegals" and "aliens" to describe persons without lawful immigration status. These terms, even when innocuously used, create division in our state and add nothing to today's immigration debate. Perhaps worse, the use of these words gives the appearance of anti-immigrant prejudice and tarnishes the image of our courts as a place where disputes may be fairly resolved. With this letter we attach a list of objectionable terms and our proposed substitutes.

What else would one call someone who is *without lawful* immigration status? And quite frankly, I believe it is the *unlawful* aspect which is at the very core of today's illegal immigration debate. Most of the people I have spoken to on this subject say more about the illegal aspect rather than the people themselves. I can't recall anyone complaining about aliens who are in this country legally.

Near the end of the above-quoted paragraph, the classic *this is going to make you look bad* approach is used when they suggest the image of the courts is being tarnished because the court used words they (Los Abogados) wish to have banned. The letter goes on to say,

> There is no place in today's immigration debate for the use of the term "illegal" to describe a person. Those supporting federal immigration reform and human rights for the undocumented uniformly declare that "no human being is illegal," but that only captures part of the issue. Nobody uses the term "illegals" to describe other people who are carrying on in their daily lives with impunity after violating the law. Persons who fail to register for Selective Service, who do not pay their taxes, who do not have a current driver's license while driving, or who violate their probation are not labeled an "illegal." Putting this in greater perspective, even a convicted murderer is never referred to as an "illegal" because of that conviction.

In this paragraph, Los Abogados, while condemning terms used by their opposition, had no problem injecting a catchphrase often used by their supporters, "no human being is illegal." The issue is not whether or not a human being is illegal, instead, it focuses on the legality of their actions and the effect those actions have on our nation.

The following is the "list of objectionable terms and our proposed substitutes" included in the letter by Los Abogados:

Immigration Terms

Immigrants

YES:	NO:
Undocumented immigrants	Illegals
Foreign nationals	Illegal aliens
Persons without legal immigration status	Aliens
Unauthorized workers	Resident or nonresident aliens
Alleged or suspected undocumented	
immigrants	Illegal immigrants
	Scratchbacks or wetbacks
	Armies of immigrants
	Invaders
	"Reconquistadores"
	Anchor babies

Immigration

YES:	NO:
Immigration debate	Illegal immigration
Immigration issue	Immigration epidemic
Immigration problem	Immigration crisis
Immigration	Immigrant invasion

Activists

YES:	NO:
Human rights advocates	Pro-illegal immigration activists
Pro-immigrant supporters	Open borders advocates
Immigration reform proponents	Illegal immigrants
Community activists	Proponents for amnesty

We've all heard of convictions being overturned on appeal because of typos in search warrants, evidence allowed or disallowed during a trial, the exact wording of court documents/testimony, and other such technicalities. The activist-created terms are, from a strictly legal standpoint, ambiguous at best. Ambiguity often creates difficulties in the prosecution process while benefiting the defense. This is one of the many reasons I am not surprised this letter was written by an organization comprised mainly of defense lawyers.

In a court of law, the term *illegal alien* is not intended as an ethnic slur; instead, it is the term officially used by the United States government to define and describe those people who are in this country without legal authorization. In short, it is the law. To avoid possible loopholes, would it not be best to stick with the actual legal terms?

So far, I have found no evidence that the Arizona Supreme Court has complied with the requests made by Los Abogados in this letter, other than forwarding it to other judges. By not using the proper and legal terms in court proceedings, people like the Chandler Rapist could conceivably be set free by the courts of appeal. Ironically, if the Arizona Supreme Court justices had complied, allowing the activist-created PC terms to create such loopholes, they would have had no choice but to overturn such convictions.

I would not have a problem with a judge disallowing the legal status of a defendant to be placed into evidence in cases where it is irrelevant—such as a murder trial—to avoid the possibility of the *anti-immigrant prejudice* Los Abogados mentioned. But in cases where such evidence is relevant, the proper terms should be used.

Regardless of their intent, it is important to point out that people who are in this country illegally are violating the federal law. In our society, we assign different names to different crimes to easily identify the differences between them. We also have different penalties for each crime. For example, a jaywalker should not be given the life sentence a murderer might, nor should we call a jaywalker a murderer. I certainly do not consider the crime of being in this country illegally to be in any way equivalent to the crime of murder. Therefore, I do not refer to the people violating immigration laws as murderers. I do consider such people to be what they truly and legally are: illegal aliens. It has nothing to do with the person being illegal, but instead, the crime that person may have committed.

Although PC is a serious problem here in the Unites States, it is also not difficult to find examples of it around the world. The following stories illustrate how PC is indeed a global problem.

In London, England, British Airways banned a Christian woman from wearing a cross on a necklace to work. Heathrow check-in worker Nadia Eweida was sent home after refusing to remove the crucifix, which breached British Airways' dress code. A duty manager ordered Eweida to remove her cross or hide it beneath a company cravat. When she requested permission from British Airways management to wear the chain, she was turned down. In response to management's refusal, Eweida said,[33]

> I will not hide my belief in the Lord Jesus. British Airways permits Muslims to wear a headscarf, Sikhs to wear a turban and other faiths religious apparel. Only Christians are forbidden to express their faith. I am a loyal and conscientious employee of British Airways, but I stand up for the rights of all citizens.

This story illustrates how political correctness can produce the opposite effect of its original intent. Modern-day PC is believed by some to have originated in Western Europe and North America. In those countries, the majority of the people with religious beliefs are Christians. In an effort to promote tolerance of, and the prevention of discrimination against minority religions in these regions, PC has actually created an anti-Christian atmosphere.

For example, it is very common for television stations to place a picture of a menorah on the screen and say "happy Hanukkah" during the Jewish holiday, but it's rare to see them show a Christmas tree and say "merry Christmas" during the Christian holiday. And for the record, it's not a holiday tree, it's a Christmas tree. Would we call a menorah a holiday candleholder? And if we did couldn't that be seen as being disrespectful and intolerant of the Jewish faith?

If a company allows or bans employees from displaying religious symbols on the job, it should be done across the board instead of discriminating against one particular religion. If we as a society are to be truly tolerant of any religious beliefs, then we should be tolerant of all religious beliefs—including Christianity. Anything less is not tolerance but is instead discrimination.

As a society, we don't seem to have a problem with allowing people to display their personalities and lifestyle choices in the form of tattoos and multicolored hair. Why then do we seem to have such a problem with simple religious symbols?

Whether it is an overreaction to the display of religious symbols or how schoolchildren interact with each other, those who give into the pressures of PC would do their jobs better by relying more on old-fashioned common sense.

A violent incident occurred in a Milford, Connecticut, middle school that put one student in the hospital prompting officials at the school to implement a "no touching" policy. A letter reportedly sent to the student's parents by the school's principal, Catherine Williams, explained, [34]

> *Observed behaviors of concern recently exhibited include kicking others in the groin area, grabbing and touching of others in personal areas, hugging and horseplay. Physical contact is prohibited to keep all students safe in the learning environment.*

> *Potential consequences and disciplinary action may include parent conferences, detention, suspension and/or a request for expulsion from school.*

Many of the students and parents were outraged believing the school's no tolerance policy went way too far, while others claimed it was *utterly ridiculous*. When considering the fact his child would no longer be allowed to do something as innocent as exchanging a *high five* or give a friend a hug, one father said,

> *Now it's almost as if it's a sanitized school. Where you have to keep your distance from everybody? And that's not what school is about.*

Another parent, Kathy Casey, brought up an interesting point, which just happened to be the first thing that popped into my mind upon reading this article:

> *What if they are out on the playground at recess, or in gym class? You know, gym class is physical.*

A "no touching" policy would tend to make the game of football a bit boring. Are the defensive players supposed to simply point at the ball carrier and say, "You're tackled"? Even some student rights activists believe these types of policies have gone too far. Derek Randel, president of StoppingSchoolViolence.com, was reported as saying,[35]

> *I see nothing wrong with hugging, if the teachers could tell the difference between good touch and bad touch whether someone is bullying or horse playing that would go much farther.*

Some people believe the policy stems from a 1999 Supreme Court decision that found school districts liable for damages in cases of peer sexual harassment. That decision was handed down because of a case where the mother of a student who was repeatedly harassed by another student filed suit against the school district that ignored the problem.

But Justice Sandra Day O'Connor warned in the court's decision that broad-based policies alone won't protect schools from lawsuits:

> *We stress that our conclusion here—that recipients may be liable for their deliberate indifference to known acts of peer sexual harassment—does not mean that recipients can avoid liability only by purging their schools of actionable peer harassment or that administrators must engage in particular disciplinary action.*

And from the *out-of-the-mouths-of-babes* category comes a similar story.

Madison Muir, a twelve-year-old seventh grader in Prattville, Alabama, was given an in-school suspension at Prattville Junior High School after giving a grieving friend a hug during a school break. When asked about the infraction, Muir replied,

> *I mean it's not like we're doing anything wrong. It's just a hug.*

Sometimes adults could learn a lot from children. Instead of automatically jumping to the most radical of solutions, wouldn't it have been better to ban physical contact only in private areas and those of a violent nature? I doubt anyone would have had a problem with that solution.

For those of you who thought my hypothetical hate crime story about the two men in a bar was unrealistic, here is a real-life story:

In Chicopee, Massachusetts, self-proclaimed witch Kelly Lynch[36] was offended by a Halloween decoration of a witch hanging from a noose. She was so offended she went to the owner's front door and asked him to take it down. The owner refused.

> "*He told me that people should lighten up, and that it's a Halloween decoration,*" said Lynch. "*To have that as your only Halloween decoration, it's kind of odd.*"

Lynch called the display a hate crime against her religion and to the entire community. Is displaying a Halloween decoration really a hate crime? It could be seen as poor taste perhaps, but a hate crime? Sometimes truth is stranger than fiction. If this kind of story can take place in the real world, is my scenario really that far-fetched? You make the call.

Not all stories about holiday characters are quite this bizarre although some still make me wonder what goes through the minds of those who have issues with them.

In Sydney, Australia, a recruitment firm warned people dressing up as Santa Claus not to say "ho, ho, ho" because it could frighten children and was too close to *ho*, a U.S. slang term for *prostitute*. Julie Gale, who runs the campaign against sexualizing children called "Kids Free 2B Kids" told a local newspaper,[37]

> *Gimme a break. We are talking about little kids who do not understand that ho, ho, ho has any other connotation and nor should they. Leave Santa alone.*

It is refreshing to know there are at least some people like Derek Randel and Julie Gale who manage to maintain their common sense.

Children who live in countries that celebrate Christmas have, for centuries, grown up with the image of that big-bellied, chubby-cheeked man known as Santa Claus—the big guy in the red-and-white suit who travels the world on Christmas eve to spread joy and happiness to all children by leaving presents under the Christmas tree. In return for his kindness and goodwill, children traditionally leave treats for Santa as a way of saying thank-you, and also to help him keep his strength during his long, hard night's work.

But Bluewater shopping center in Greenhithe, Kent, UK, apparently has decided jolly ol' Saint Nick is setting a bad example for today's children by being too fat. So they decided to send their shopping center Santas to boot camp to trim down. Fiona Campbell-Reilly, speaking for the shopping center, said,[38]

> *Santa has been around for years, but society has changed and our Santa needs to reflect this. Bluewater's Santa Boot Camp is getting Santa in shape and setting a good example to children who idolize him. He will still be the same lovable jolly man, but will be fitter and healthier.*

There are certain truths in this world: fire burns, water is wet, and Santa Claus is fat. I can't recall a single moment in my childhood when I thought, "Gee, when I grow up, I want to be a big fat guy just like Santa."

However, in the interest of being fair, I conducted an unscientific poll of some of today's kids to see if perhaps things have changed since the dinosaur days of my youth. When asked if they thought Santa should go to the gym and shed a few pounds, almost without exception they replied, "No way! Santa is supposed to be fat."

When asked if they wanted to be fat like Santa when they grew up, the most common response was, "What? Are you stupid? Of course not!" Again, from the mouths of babes we find wisdom and common sense.

I am happy to report that Bluewater's management need not worry about the children of today. They will be just fine. I also wish to second Julie Gale's eloquently stated, "Gimme a break! Leave Santa alone." I have actually seen a slim and trim Santa Claus, and for the record, it just looked weird.

Unfortunately, Christmas and Halloween are not the only holidays to have their traditions assaulted by the PC crowd.

For four decades, two kindergarten schools in Claremont, California, have had a tradition of sharing a Thanksgiving feast just before the holiday break. In this tradition, students from each school dress in construction paper costumes. Each year the students from one school dress as Pilgrims and the students from the other as Indians. The costumes alternate between schools annually. But this four-decade-long tradition may be coming to an end because of PC.[39]

Michelle Raheja, the mother of a kindergartner at Condit Elementary School, reportedly wrote a letter to her daughter's teacher complaining about the tradition, stating,

> It's demeaning. I'm sure you can appreciate the inappropriateness of asking children to dress up like slaves (and kind slave masters), or Jews (and friendly Nazis), or members of any other racial minority group who has struggled in our nation's history.

Raheja, an English professor at the University of California Riverside who specializes in Native American literature, said she wished to see alternatives that celebrate thankfulness without *dehumanizing* her daughter's ancestry.

"*There is nothing to be served by dressing up as a racist stereotype,*" she said.

District Superintendent David Cash announced at the end of a school board meeting before the annual event that the two schools had tentatively decided to hold the event without the costumes. Many of the school's parents believe that the decision was made before the board meeting and accused administrators of bowing to the pressures of PC.

Kathleen Lucas, who is of Choctaw heritage, said her son still wears the vest and feathered headband he made the previous year.

My son was so proud. In his eyes, he thinks that's what it looks like to be Indian.

Constance Garabedian, a mother of one of the kindergartners apparently accused Raheja of using those children as a political platform for herself and her ideas.

> *I'm not a professor and I'm not a historian, but I can put the dots together.*

Another parent said,

> *She's* [Raheja] *not going to tell us what we can and cannot wear. We're tired of* [district officials] *cowing down to people. It's not right.*

Jennifer Tilton, an assistant professor of race and ethnic studies at the University of Redlands and a Claremont parent who opposes the costumes stated,

> *It's always a good thing to think about, critically, how we teach kids, even from very young ages, the message we want them to learn, and the respect for the diversity of the American experiences.*

In principle, I do agree with that statement. But let's take a closer look at what these students are celebrating and a closer look at what I believe it teaches them.

On November 9, 1620, the Pilgrims ended a two-month-long journey to the New World. They had originally intended to settle in Virginia where they hoped to start a new life free to practice their religion. But violent autumn storms blew their ship—the *Mayflower*—off course, and they eventually landed in Massachusetts instead. Because they arrived in unfamiliar territory in early winter, it became very difficult for them to find food and build shelter. Many settlers did not survive the first few months.

Fortunately for the settlers, an Indian tribe called Wampanoag already lived in the Massachusetts Bay area. They shared their knowledge of local crops and navigation with the Pilgrims and helped them survive. In 1621, the Wampanoag and Pilgrims came together for a three-day feast to celebrate their first year of cooperation and interaction and to give thanks for what they had. Although there is some dispute, many historians look at this event as being the first occurrence of what we now call Thanksgiving.

Since that era, the various tribes of American Indians have been treated extremely poorly, not only by other settlers but also eventually by the United States government as well. To give a few examples, they had their lands stolen from them, many were wrongfully imprisoned, and some tribes were slaughtered almost, if not in fact, to the point of extinction.

But it is not those atrocities that these students celebrate. Instead, they celebrate a time of peaceful coexistence—a time when people from different races, cultures, spiritual beliefs, and entirely different worlds came together for one common cause: survival.

It is also important to note that this celebration is being shared by two different schools. These schools, which otherwise might be rivals, are instead working together for common goals. I believe they are learning tolerance, understanding, and the development of friendships with peers from other schools through peaceful cooperation. I fail to see how this practice could be seen as demeaning, dehumanizing, or as a racist stereotype.

Might someone be offended because the costumes the students create may not be historically accurate? These children are kindergartners, not Hollywood costume designers. Or is it simply another case of overactive PC to serve a particular agenda?

Like Constance Garabedian, I am neither a professor or a historian. But I would venture to guess that back in those early days of our nation's history, it was most likely the then politically correct mentality of racial, cultural, and religious superiority that led to the persecution of Indian tribes in the first place.

As I said before, political correctness is not only the use of kinder and gentler words to protect the sensitivities of others. It is also used to manipulate the minds of the masses to further the sometimes horrible agendas of a few. Those who took advantage of American Indians created an atmosphere of paranoia and fear to justify their actions. Not that Michelle Raheja's concerns necessarily fall into that category, but I do think we should not penalize these children simply for the sake of the misguided politically correct views of a few.

From kindergartens to colleges, political correctness has created a distorted view of American Indian heritage and the respect many people have for them.

In 2006, the National Collegiate Athletic Association (NCAA) ruled the two feathers that appear on the William & Mary College's athletic logo are "hostile and abusive" to American Indians. Gene Nichol, then president of William & Mary, sent an e-mail to the student body saying the college would not pursue legal action to appeal the decision.

In 2007, the college also warned student groups that any parade float entry violating the following policy would be rejected:[40]

> Showcasing a Native American or Native American symbols will not be allowed to participate. The unit entry application will be rejected and the unit will not be able to walk the parade route.

Upon hearing of the NCAA's ruling, and the college's apparent willingness to give into such pressure, Joe Luppino-Esposito, a board member of the chapter of the Young Americans for Freedom at the college, said,

> This is political correctness run amok. But even so, this is not even a left-right issue. This is common sense. Two feathers are not offensive, and anyone who thinks so should not be taken seriously.

The NCAA ruling was condemned by many students associated with YAF, a nonpartisan organization that has both liberal and conservative views. To protest the ruling, members of the YAF distributed twenty-five thousand feathers during the homecoming game to students and alumni. In response to the protest, Luppino-Esposito said,

> I am glad that we have the opportunity to help show our love for the college and our team and also send a message to the NCAA that despite their official actions, there is nothing they can [do to] stop us from using the symbols we want to use.

Correct me if I am wrong, but when school athletic programs choose mascots or symbols to represent their institutions and their teams, they usually choose something they respect and which also illustrates their commitment to athletic excellence.

For example, a bear is a powerful animal quite capable of defending itself. An eagle is a proud majestic bird that can soar high in the sky for hours in search of prey. American Indians have historically demonstrated their amazing ability to survive and prosper in unforgiving and hostile environments. Many tribes developed cultures based on honor, strong spiritual values, and a deep respect for nature and humanity. I fail to see how the NCAA (or anyone else) can view a respectful representation of such noble people as hostile and abusive.

Is this just an example of William & Mary College bowing down to PC pressure from the NCAA or does it go deeper than this story reveals? Is there a deeper hidden agenda? Political correctness can be used to force people not only to abandon symbols, mascots, and tradition, but it can also and often is used to attempt to destroy our core beliefs.

In 2005, East Brunswick New Jersey High School adopted a policy prohibiting representatives of the school district from participating in student-initiated prayer.[41] Under the new policy, they ordered Marcus Borden, the school's head football coach, to not bow his head while the players on his team prayed for the safety of each other and their opponents prior to each game. The school claimed that while they could not legally prevent students from praying if they chose, it could stop any recognition of that act by coaches because they are public employees and their participation would violate the so-called *separation of church and state* clause of the First Amendment. In an interview with a Denver television station, Coach Border said,

> *We're teaching kids values in the game of football. There's nothing wrong with being spiritual . . . I just asked to be able to be respectful of my team.*

When Coach Borden went to court to appeal the school's decision, District Judge Dennis Cavanaugh declared that in its attempt to halt Coach Borden from either silently bowing his head or taking a knee while the players prayed, the district violated his rights to free speech, freedom of association, and academic freedom.

The school district, with the assistance of Americans United for Separation of Church and State, argued in its appeal to Judge Cavanaugh's decision that the coach did not have a constitutional right of expression or academic freedom. Apparently, the Third U.S. Circuit Court of Appeals agreed by concluding that the First Amendment does not protect such expressive conduct.

Coach Borden told the Denver television station he planned to appeal that decision to the United States Supreme Court. The U.S. Supreme Court hears only a fraction of the cases submitted and has the right to refuse to hear his appeal. If they refuse to hear this case, the decision of the Third U.S. Circuit Court of Appeals would stand.

John W. Whitehead, president of the Rutherford Institute who has worked on the case, said,

> *If this ruling is allowed to stand, it will mean that high school teachers across the United States will have no free speech or academic freedom rights at all. This undermines a time-honored tradition that has less to do with religion than it does athletic tradition. It's a sad statement on our rights as Americans that schools are no longer bastions of freedom. We've become so politically correct and secularized that religious individuals who seek the same First Amendment rights as others are censored.*

To further understand how two courts interpreting the same laws can arrive at two different conclusions, we should understand court *decisions* are just that—decisions of the justices involved. We must then look at exactly what the law states and how it can be interpreted in different manners. The First Amendment of the Constitution of the United States reads,

> *Congress shall make no law respecting an establishment of religion, or prohibiting the free exercise thereof; or abridging the freedom of speech, or of the press, or the right of the people peaceably to assemble, and to petition the Government for a redress of grievances.*

But what do the first two clauses really mean? In my opinion, the first clause—*respecting an establishment of religion*—means the government cannot establish a national religion, or create laws that openly support the doctrine of any one religion. Does this mean representatives of our government are not allowed to be respectful of religious faiths? No. Both the first and second clauses—*and prohibiting the free exercise thereof*—were designed to protect and respect the rights of the people to have and practice their religious beliefs free from government *interference*. They were not designed to require our government to ignore its very existence.

I wish to make it clear; I do support separation of church and state. We have seen the dangers of church-run nations throughout history. Many of these nations have been responsible for some of the worst examples of man's inhumanity to man. The ancient Egyptian's attempt at world dominance and its enslavement of the conquered, the Spanish Inquisition, and the British-led Crusades are just a few that come to mind. And let's not forget a few Islamic-led nations that (historically and currently) not only support terrorist activities but also provide direct assistance to terrorists in the form of financial support, training facilities, and weapons.

When nations allow their governments to be directly (or indirectly) run by an organized religion, they greatly limit (or eliminate entirely) the freedoms of the people in those nations. The church, which controls these nations, will often strongly discourage, or outright forbid the practice of any other religion by its citizens. These legal restrictions will often extend to the expression of any resistance to the ruling church doctrine. Some of the laws of these nations go so far as to make it a crime to violate church doctrine.

When our founding fathers wrote the Declaration of Independence and the Constitution, they did so in an effort to free themselves and the people of this new nation from the tyranny of a monarch who was also the leader of the national church. They wished to create a nation where its citizens would have the freedom to establish different religions and the freedom to practice their chosen faith without government oppression. In short, they created an atmosphere where all religions were welcome and the rights of those who wish to practice them were not only respected but also protected.

Opponents to prayer in school claim that if Coach Borden participates in any way, his actions could be seen as coercion by those players who don't wish to pray, and is therefore a violation of the law. But remember, the prayers were initiated by the players, not the coach. That means the players were engaging in prayer of their own free will.

The way I see it, if Coach Borden had initiated, pressured, or ordered his players to engage in prayer, he would then be in violation of the First Amendment. Bowing his head or taking a knee on the sidelines is not coercion, it is called respect. If anyone is following another's lead, it is the coach who is following the players.

And while you consider this case and the arguments I have presented, keep in mind the rights Coach Borden possesses in regard to freedom of religion as well as freedom of expression of his faith. By issuing their ruling, the Third U.S. Circuit Court of Appeals told him he has no legal right to pray with or around his team, or to even respect his team's right to pray because he is employed by a government entity. Could this not be seen as a form of discrimination or even a violation of constitutional law?

Those who possess strong religious convictions live their lives with those convictions around the clock. They should not be ordered by the government to place their beliefs on hold because of who issues their paychecks. This is a case where the government itself is in violation of the First Amendment by prohibiting the free exercise of religion. It is also yet another example of political correctness run amok in order to carry out an apparent hidden agenda.

CHAPTER SEVEN

The Shell Game

Government is not reason; it is not eloquent; it is force.
Like fire, it is a dangerous servant and a fearful master.

—George Washington

S ome of us have either seen or have been a victim of the simple con known as the shell game and therefore familiar with its premise. For those of you who are not familiar with it, I'll give the basics of how it works.

The person running the game will show you three shells, or something similar, and a small ball. They will tell you the object of the game is really quite simple explaining that they will place the ball under one of the shells, shuffle the shells around, and all you need to do is keep track of the shell under which the ball is hidden. They demonstrate the simplicity of the game by placing the ball under one shell, slowly shuffling the shells so it is easy for you to keep your eye on the correct shell, and then ask you to pick the correct shell when they stop shuffling.

Once you're convinced of how simple keeping track of the ball is, they ask if you want to try again, but this time place a wager on whether or not you can again choose the correct shell. If you agree to place the wager, the game suddenly becomes more difficult.

The shells are again shuffled, but this time, much quicker. You continue to track the shell you saw the ball placed under, but this time, the ball is not there. Through sleight of hand, the person shuffling the shells removes the ball and places it in the palm of their hand out of your view. Once you choose the shell you believe the ball is under, the con artist lifts that shell (which, of course, has no ball), then places the ball under another shell while you are distracted. The con artist will then pick up the shell that does contain the ball to *prove* to you it was there all along, and you lost track of it. It is a simple game as you were originally informed, but what they don't tell you is it is also a game you simply can't win. That is, unless you know what to look for.

Once you realize the shell game is nothing more than a con job, you can stay and be robbed of your hard-earned money, or you can refuse to be taken in by it and walk away. With this con, you have the choice. In the political shell game, the choice is usually left to others. When this con is run, it is not always just money we stand to lose but our rights as well. For an example of this, I will continue the story of Coach Borden.

Those who spend a great deal of time and money fighting people like Coach Borden claim they do so to protect and preserve our constitutional rights. They portray themselves as gallant warriors protecting us and our children against those who wish to unlawfully influence us. I think most of these groups have a much different agenda and are more concerned with the abolishment of religious freedoms than protecting them. Even though most of these groups claim to be nonpartisan, they often speak of fighting the views of the *religious right*, while apparently supporting views commonly held by the left. That sounds far too one-sided to be called nonpartisan to me.

But what about the high school football players these people claim to be so gallantly protecting? How do they feel about this case? In an *amicus curiae* (friend of the court) brief prepared by the American Football Coaches Association and filed with the U.S. Supreme Court requesting them to hear this case, we can find insight to these questions:[42]

Indeed, even a coach who stands by stoically while his players pray could be accused of monitoring whether players are participating, thereby improperly "coercing" reluctant team members to join those team leaders who initiate the prayer. See Lee v. Weisman, 505 U.S. 577, 590, 592-593 (1992) (school officials, by monitoring student prayer, can cause the "subtle" or "indirect" coercive pressure that is constitutionally forbidden). The most constitutionally sound practice, apparently, is to walk out on one's players.

Walking out, of course, could be construed as reasonably communicating a message of disapproval or hostility toward religion, which this Court says is also inconsistent with the Establishment Clause. See Lynch v. Donnelly,

465 U.S. 668, 673 (1984). The record in this case (specifically, the joint appendix filed in the Third Circuit) reveals that Coach Borden's players felt awkward and uncomfortable during the 2005 season when their coaches would freeze during player-initiated prayers. J.A. 169; 440-442. The players believed it hurt team morale. J.A. 169.

Because this Court has condemned governmental conduct having the primary effect of advancing or inhibiting religion, see Lemon v. Kurtzman, 403 U.S. 602, 612-613 (1971), surely the sensitivity of students to what reasonably appears to be governmental hostility to religion is as constitutionally significant as the sensitivity of students to what reasonably appears to be governmental endorsement of religion.

The AFCA has a valid point. If Coach Borden is coercing his team to support religious activities by bowing his head or taking a knee, then it could be said that the Third U.S. Circuit Court of Appeals is coercing Coach Borden's team against religious activities by forcing their coach to turn his back on them. And who will protect us from the coercive activities of the Third U.S. Circuit Court of Appeals, which is, just in case it hasn't struck you, a government entity? Kind of ironic, don't you think?

Instead of hearing this hotly debated and precedent-setting case to set the appropriate standards by which all such matters would be judged, in the spring of 2009, the Supreme Court officially refused to hear Coach Borden's appeal. Apparently, the United States Supreme Court decided the best course of action in this case was to simply avoid the issue entirely.

We should not be surprised by this. Federal judges and Supreme Court justices are not elected officials and are allowed to serve for the remainder of their lives if they so choose, providing they "hold their offices during good behavior." This means that once in office, they are basically accountable to no one. When a vacancy in the court occurs, federal judges and Supreme Court justices are appointed by the current sitting president, with senate approval. On the surface, that may sound like a fair and nonpartisan way of selecting a replacement. Far too often, however, this is not the case.

If the sitting president has liberal views, and the senate is comprised of mostly liberals, then any justice appointed by the president and approved by the senate will most likely share the same liberal views. If the balance of power is in favor of conservatives, then the appointee will most likely be a conservative.

Granting no system is perfect, I believe an appointee approach to determining our federal judges and Supreme Court justices was one of the few mistakes made by our founding fathers when they wrote the Constitution—although understandable given the communication challenges at the time.

These offices should be held by those who are duly elected by majority vote of the people with terms of office in place and subject to reelection (or not) by the people. This way, the people who sit in judgment of us, our way of life, and most importantly our Constitution would be accountable for how they judge.

They would also be more likely to make rulings based on the true intent of our founding fathers rather than the advancement of their own political party's agenda—in other words, make judgments on constitutional law based on common sense instead of political paybacks or ideology. Even this system would not be perfect, but it would certainly be a more fair and accountable one instead of the political shell game the current system has become.

Again, my personal agenda is to convince people not to trust the first thing they read or hear, but to think for themselves. President Obama has said that if someone wants to know what he is all about, they should look at the people he surrounds himself with. That is very sound advice, which we should all take when searching for the truth. Whom a person befriends or associates with often reveals a great deal about that person. When it comes to a politician's associations, it says even more.

Many politicians are very good at telling people what they want to hear. If you want proof of this, follow almost any politician around during their campaign and see how different their speeches are depending on the groups they address. They will often tell labor unions one thing and business executives another. Police officers may be promised better tools to fight crime, while defense attorneys are promised legislation designed to make it easier to defend their clients. They usually say whatever it takes to whomever it takes to get elected. That is how the political shell game begins.

When our country began, our founding fathers provided sufficient time for elections to take place, votes to be counted and verified, and enough time for the newly elected officials to travel to their respective locations to carry out their duties (federal and state capitals, etc.). Back then, a person couldn't catch a red-eye and travel across the country overnight as is possible today. We still maintain these time spans between elections and oaths of office today. Some say it should remain because it allows sufficient time for a smooth transition of power when one official replaces another. I suspect it also allows sufficient time for voters to forget the campaign promises made to them before the election.

Many Americans believe that once in office, most politicians eventually become overwhelmed by the pressures of special interest groups, lobbyists, and the agendas of their own political parties. They also believe that even the newly elected officials who truly have a desire to change the things they believe to be wrong with our system, in time become corrupted by that system.

Politicians who allow themselves to become corrupted get the promise of votes from special interest groups, campaign contributions and *gifts* from lobbyists, as well as political favors from other party members in office through the *you scratch my back and I'll scratch yours* method of conducting business. The only ones left out of this equation are the voters who put them into office in the first place. But do we as voters have the right to complain?

We elect these people, send them off to represent us, then go back to our regular lives and forget about them and what they do. We watch the evening news or read newspapers and think we are getting accurate reports. We fool ourselves into thinking that if something worth paying attention to happens, the news media will inform us and we can deal with it then.

Most Americans are familiar with system of *checks and balances* our founding fathers set up for the federal government—the three separate but equal branches known as the legislative, executive, and judicial. They also set up a similar system to protect us *from* the federal government: state's rights (the Tenth Amendment), the people's rights (First and Tenth Amendments), and the freedom of the press (First Amendment) just to name a few. The press was given so much freedom—and power—so they could keep an eye on government at all levels to help prevent corruption as well as to expose corruption when it did occur.

But is the news media in this country giving us the accurate story? Are they giving us an unbiased story? Don't make the mistake of only having one or two sources for news. If you are one of those who do limit your news sources, I can almost guarantee you that you are *not* being told the whole truth; and in most cases, you are being mislead and/or lied to. And in what seems to be an ever-increasing scenario, sometimes you are not being given the story at all. That is a lesson I learned the hard way during the course of research for this book.

While doing research, too many times I would come across a story from one major media source—which I felt was more than worthy of national media attention—then I would go to another source to get a different perspective only to find the second source wasn't covering the story at all. In some cases if—and only after the story had become too big to ignore—the second source did begin covering the story, it was only to criticize the first source for covering the story in the first place. I found these practices disturbing to say the least.

Why would any credible major news outlet refuse to cover major news stories, to begin with, and then launch attacks on another for breaking the story? Is it because they didn't want the story to be told? Is it because of a vast difference of opinion by the different news outlets on what constitutes a worthy news story? Or is it because many in the media have become more interested in spreading propaganda that matches their own political beliefs and the agendas of those politicians who share those beliefs?

In the days of my youth, we didn't have the Internet. We had no choice but to trust the press to be our watchdogs, which is why they were given so much freedom in the constitution. But with that freedom comes the responsibility of not only telling the story, but also telling the whole story in a truthful manner and allowing the people to decide what, if anything, needs to be done. Unfortunately, many in the press have gone from being watchdogs for the people to being lapdogs for politicians.

What it comes down to is that each of us as citizens and patriots must become watchdogs for this country. We must take the time to find multiple sources for news. We must question any and everything that has even the slightest ring of political correctness to it. In short, protecting this country and our American way of life has fallen to us—each and every one of us. Don't be discouraged by the old trick of, "You can never get that many people to get on the same page."

In fact, don't worry about what everyone else is doing at all. Start the process in your own life. Don't be afraid to speak out when you know something you are being told is wrong. Don't sit by in silence because you are too afraid of being called names or appear unintelligent because your views don't match the PC dogma; that dogma is wrong and should be challenged.

Once you start doing it, others will be inspired by your courage to speak the truth and will join with you. Before you know it, this practice will soon spread like wildfire. With the advantage of the Internet, the last true avenue of free speech, we no longer have any excuses for not being informed about the world around us. Start using it before it too becomes controlled and restricted by those who wish to control your thoughts. But your responsibility doesn't stop there.

When was the last time you contacted your representative or senators in Congress to let them know how you felt on an issue which was important to you? When was the last time you actually checked to see how your representative or senators in Congress voted on an issue which was important to you? When was the last time you actually checked to see how your representative or senators in Congress voted on *any* issue? If you are like most in this country, your answer would be *never*. In fact, most people do not even know the names of the people in Congress who represent them.

Because we don't let our representatives know how we feel, we the people are *not* the proverbial squeaky wheels. We, therefore, often get overlooked when lawmakers set policy, and we have no one to blame but ourselves. Obviously, we can no longer solely rely on the press to do it for us, and our politicians are very much aware of this. The political shell game becomes effective when politicians know we're not keeping our eyes on them (the ball) while they advance their agendas hidden under politically correct shells.

For a case in point, we only need to go back to the discussion between one of Obama's economic advisers, Robert Reich, and U.S. representative Charlie Rangel, Democrat from New York. During testimony broadcast on C-SPAN, on January 7, 2009, before the House Ways and Means Committee—the committee that Representative Rangel chairs—Reich explained his views on how stimulus money earmarked for infrastructure should be distributed, as well as to whom:[43]

> *I am concerned, as I'm sure many of you are, that these jobs not simply go to high-skilled people who are already professionals or to white male construction workers . . . I have nothing against white male construction workers, I'm just saying there are other people who have needs as well. And therefore, in my remarks I have suggested to you, and I'm certainly happy to talk about it more, ways in which the money can be—criteria can be set so that the money does go to others: the long-term unemployed, minorities, women, people who are not necessarily construction workers or high-skilled professionals.*

Critics of Reich's remarks later claimed he was suggesting that *no* white male construction workers should be hired. After reading text of the testimony and Reich's comments posted on his own blog (published January 8, 2009), I have come to the conclusion that these accusations are not true. He did recommend establishing criteria (or quotas) that would force contractors to provide at least 20 percent of the jobs to people in these groups who have very little, or in most cases, absolutely no training. He also suggests 2 percent of the monies allocated for each project should be used to train these workers:

> I'd suggest that all contracts entered into with stimulus funds require contractors to provide at least 20 percent of jobs to the long-term unemployed and to people with incomes at or below 200 percent of the federal poverty level. And at least 2 percent of project funds should be allocated to such training.

What kind of projects are we talking about? In his blog, Reich explains,[44]

> The stimulus plan will create jobs repairing and upgrading the nation's roads, bridges, ports, levees, water and sewage system, public-transit systems, electricity grid, and schools. And it will kick-start alternative, non-fossil based sources of energy (wind, solar, geothermal, and so on); new health-care information systems; and universal broadband Internet access. But there's no reason to think about "green jobs" as simply high-tech. Many low-income and low-skilled workers—women as well as men—could be put directly to work providing homes and businesses with more efficient and renewable heating, lighting, cooling, and refrigeration systems; installing solar panels and efficient photovoltaic systems; rehabilitating and renovating old properties; and improving recycling systems.

> "Green Jobs Corps" teams could be trained to evaluate and advise homeowners and businesses on these and other means of conserving energy.

So if I understand what Reich is saying, the United States government should demand that low-skilled and non-skilled workers should be immediately put to work, not only in smaller jobs working with electrical components and systems which (without extensive and proper training) could easily kill them, but also repairing, improving, and building systems vital to public safety and national security. According to him, however, these workers could be trained to do these jobs in a relatively short period of time:

> People can be trained relatively quickly for these sorts of jobs, as well as many infrastructure jobs generated by the stimulus—installing new pipes for water and sewage systems, repairing and upgrading equipment, basic construction—but contractors have to be nudged both to provide the training and to do the hiring.

Reich also suggests the government (in other words, we the taxpayers) should pay the salaries of these groups while they train:[45]

> Provide income assistance during training. One of the biggest barriers for vulnerable populations who want such training is their need for income: while being trained. Income maintenance should be assured for the duration of training, up to six months.

Apparently, Dr. Reich has never heard of on-the-job training in conjunction with night classes. Unfortunately, some people would take advantage of being paid to attend training classes just for the income. Once the classes (and the income) end, they would have no interest in actually working in the field. With on-the-job training, at least the taxpayer would be getting some actual work done for their money. And those who are serious about working would still be employed after six months. I have been through many excellent classes designed to prepare me to work in the electrical trade, but none of those classes gave me the quality of experience and training I received from hands-on experience in the field.

Reich may know a great deal about money, but if he truly believes what he is saying, he is grossly out of touch with how things actually work in the building trades. And this man was once the U.S. secretary of labor? I shouldn't be surprised though; I'm talking about a political position in Washington DC after all.

I have worked in the construction field as an electrician for the better part of thirty years. During my career, I worked on residential, commercial, governmental, and industrial projects with union and nonunion contractors. Both union and nonunion contractors typically attempt to man their projects primarily with skilled craftsmen. But they also understand the value and importance of training apprentices to maintain an adequate level of skilled craftsmen for future projects. In this area, Reich's plan makes sense: training unskilled workers.

One of the three main problems with his plan is the naive notion you can take someone who knows nothing about a trade and adequately train them in a short period of time, especially in only six months as he suggests. Another is that his plan places far too many completely unskilled apprentices into the system at once. And lastly, it creates the very real possibility that, not only will some white men be stripped of the opportunity to get these jobs, but also some minorities and women who are already skilled craftsmen and apprentices will be shut out as well.

Inadequate training: Most apprenticeship programs in the building trades last either four or five years. Again, using the electrical trade as an example, to become a fully qualified electrician, a person must study and learn building codes, national and sometimes state electrical codes, as well as federal and state safety standards. All these must be learned in addition to learning the trade itself, which involves several different and ever-changing aspects. I have met hundreds of electricians who have spent thirty years or more in the trade and have told me they are still learning the trade. Simply put, you can't just grab some wire, throw it into a wall, and call it good. Almost all the other building trades face similar issues.

Unskilled apprentices: Wise contractors engage in the practice of ensuring their apprenticeship workforce is comprised of apprentices from all levels of training from the *greenhorn* to those who are about to complete their training. As is often the case, many of the higher level apprentices are (under proper supervision) allowed to work with entry level or early year apprentices as if they were already journeymen. This allows the advanced apprentice to receive training on how to properly work with and train apprentices during a time when they still fully understand what it is like to be an apprentice. This practice ensures better quality of workmanship as well as an increased level of proper training in all aspects of the trade.

Unfortunately, I have also been on projects where the contractor took this concept and attempted to man the jobs with much larger numbers of apprentices in an effort to keep labor costs down. Without fail, these projects were riddled with mistakes, which, if caught at all, had to be corrected. The incorrectly done work first had to be torn out then reworked correctly, which cost the contractor large sums of money in extra time, labor, and material. Far too often, these contractors found themselves losing millions by the time they completed the projects.

If infrastructure projects are managed in this manner, it will not only be the contractor who loses money but it will also be the taxpayers footing the bill for those mistakes. And that is not even mentioning the danger to the general public those mistakes present, discovered or not.

Do we really want such important systems repaired, maintained, and/or built by such a large number of unqualified workers? The reason for having strict building codes is to ensure the construction of such things as homes, office buildings, roads, and bridges are done in the proper way, with the safety of those who use them in mind.

Unintended discrimination: Most contractors do not like the added cost and restrictions of additional regulations and quotas. They tend to resent what they see as mandated distractions and delays in achieving their goals of getting the job done quickly and safely while ensuring the highest profit levels possible. While it is true that the skilled construction workforce in this country is still mainly comprised of white males, there are an ever-increasing number of minority and female workers who are just as qualified as their white male counterparts. Some contractors may decide to stage a silent protest by not hiring qualified minority or female workers because they feel they have met their *quotas* for hiring other groups who they feel have been forced upon them.

The only way the government could avoid these silent protests is to award the contracts on what is known as a cost-plus basis. A cost-plus contract means the contractor is reimbursed for all costs accrued during the planning and construction phases of the project plus a percentage of those overall costs as profit. On cost-plus projects, contractors like to drive the initial cost as high as possible to increase their profits in the end. On infrastructure projects this would, of course, drive the overall cost higher for the taxpayer. As I said before, Reich does know a great deal about money. But apparently he also knows a lot of ways to waste taxpayer's money.

Faced with all this, what was Representative Rangel's response to Reich's plan? Not only did he agree with Reich but he also went further by suggesting state governors should be forced to accept the mandated criteria so that contracts could not be held up in state legislatures. In reference to this ideal, Rangel said,[46]

Remove the discretion! Identify the "need." Do numbers.

Rangel also apparently reassured Reich that he need not worry about backlash from the working middle class when he said,

> *And one thing you can depend on, you don't have to be worried about what the middle-class is gonna [sic] do. Things are so bad. They have to put food on their tables. Clothes for their kids. Get them in school. I think this is a tremendous opportunity for a stronger America.*

This plan will create a stronger America, Representative Rangel? I would ask stronger for whom? I do believe we need to spend the appropriate amount of money to repair, maintain, and further develop our infrastructure. I also believe that doing so will create new jobs and help to stimulate the economy and improve the lives of thousands of Americans.

I do not believe spending additional billions (above what is appropriate) of taxpayer dollars in a manner that will weaken our vital infrastructure creates a stronger America. If these people "who have needs also" want to work on infrastructure projects, let them fill out job applications just like everyone else. Or let them join labor unions and be sent to work by apprenticeship directors in a fair and equal manner. After all, that is exactly what the minorities and women who are already working as highly skilled craftsmen did; and they did it on their own, not through some government-mandated handout.

But, Representative Rangel, if you still insist on issuing mandates, then mandate tax breaks for contractors who hire and *properly* provide training to these groups—unlike yet another government (taxpayer) supported entity such as Green Jobs Corps that will spend more money in administrative costs than training of any kind.

And one last thought: if you had bothered to check out the latest unemployment rates, you would have known a large portion of middle-class people—those whom you seem to be so unworried about finding out what you are up to—are sitting at home reading the news on the Internet while they look for jobs. And some of them even watch C-SPAN.

While reading about this exchange, did you notice the sleight of hand in this shell game? Most of the controversy in the media over this exchange was focused on the apparent so-called reverse discrimination against *white male construction workers*. For the record, there is no such thing as reverse discrimination. Discrimination is discrimination, regardless of the color of the skin of those being discriminated against.

Because the discrimination factor was so controversial, very little was mentioned about the apparent attempt to create yet another taxpayer-funded entitlement program for women, minorities, and the poor, or the apparent attempt to lay the foundation of the Obama administration's *Green Economy* agenda. If we as taxpayers are going to be forced to play the political shell game, it is up to us to keep our eye on the ball.

This rule applies not only to how our money is spent but also on who is appointed to presidential cabinets and why.

When President Obama chose former Arizona Democratic governor Janet Napolitano to be the secretary of homeland security, his administration praised her as a border state governor who was tough on border security and reducing illegal immigration. To back up this claim, they pointed to her tough stance on enforcing current immigration laws and her record of signing into law legislation designed to strengthen those laws during her terms as governor. In fact, she did sign one of the toughest bills in the nation regarding illegal immigration. But some Republican Arizona legislators claim she did so only because of intense political pressure. So what is the truth? To answer this question, let us take a look at what she has said on the subject, and what she has actually done.

The bill that then governor Napolitano signed into Arizona State law was similar to one she vetoed the previous year.[47] She signed the new bill with reservations, to say the least. Ms. Napolitano has often said primary law enforcement efforts should be placed, not on illegal aliens, but on those who employ them. After signing the bill into law, she proclaimed it to be "the most aggressive action in the country" against such employers. She was correct.

So why did she have an apparent change of heart? Since Governor Napolitano had already proven her tendency to veto similar legislation, Republican legislators threatened to overturn her veto on this bill if the new law suffered the same fate. State governors tend not to enjoy the bad press of having their vetoes overturned. It also gave Napolitano a chance to play both sides of the fence. Even though she did sign the bill, she claimed the bill was flawed and called for a special session of the legislature to amend certain provisions before the law took effect.

She found the financing in the bill "woefully inadequate" regarding enforcement of the law. She was also concerned about the absence of any statutory protection against discrimination by race or national origin, which is, of course, already protected by state and federal law. She also claimed she was forced to sign the bill because Congress had just defeated an immigration reform bill a few days before:

*Because of Congress' failure to act, states like Arizona have
no choice but to take strong action to discourage the further
flow of illegal immigration through our borders.*

Then she seemed to revert back to her apparent pro immigrant
stance by saying,

*For years now, I have spoken out on the desperate need for
comprehensive immigration reform. Today, I renew my call
on Congress to enact such legislation. The United States
Congress has a responsibility to act swiftly and definitively
to solve this problem on the national level.*

If you look at what she did as opposed to what she said, signing
legislation she apparently opposed only because of political pressure,
you may come to the conclusion that Napolitano was appointed as
DHS secretary not because she actually has a tough stance on border
security and reducing illegal immigration as suggested, but because
she gave the appearance of such.

Whether it is immigration reform or health-care reform,
politicians love to play shell games because they know it is so easy
to distract the public by making them believe the ball is somewhere
it is not.

President Obama and some Democrats in Congress have
repeatedly said no illegal aliens would benefit from important
programs Democrats were pushing through Congress. But
congressional Democrats also repeatedly defeated amendments to
these bills which stated in a clear and concise manner that no one
who is in the United States illegally would benefit from these bills
once they become law.

Democratic Senate Majority Leader Harry Reid blocked an
amendment that would require *E-Verification* of citizenship for
anyone receiving money from the stimulus package before it was
passed by Congress shortly after President Obama took office.[48]
Similar amendments requiring E-Verification have been blocked by
democratic committee chairs on other bills where illegal aliens had

RonWalker

the potential to benefit through loopholes. So if the Democrats in Congress have no intention of allowing illegal aliens to benefit from these programs, why do they oppose language in the bills ensuring that wouldn't happen?

Confused? Don't be. Just remember the old adage, which states, "Actions speak louder than words." And in this political shell game, I suggest keeping your eye on the ball instead of the shell.

Many of you may remember Congressman Joe Wilson yelling "you lie!" during President Obama's speech before a joint session of Congress when the president again claimed no illegal alien would benefit from the health-care reform bill. Was Congressman Wilson right? Did the president lie? I could argue that the president misled Congress and the American people, but I cannot say he outright lied.

In a speech to the Congressional Hispanic Caucus Institute in September 2009 regarding the then-proposed health-care reform bill, President Obama said,[49]

> I want to be clear. If someone is here illegally they won't be covered under this plan. A commitment I've made. But I also want to make this clear. Even though I do not believe we can extend coverage to those who are here illegally, I also don't simply believe we can simply ignore the fact that our immigration system is broken. That's why I strongly support making sure folks who are here legally have access to affordable, quality health insurance under this plan, just like everybody else. If anything, this debate underscores the necessity of passing comprehensive immigration reform and resolving the issue of 12 million undocumented people living and working in this country once and for all. That's what I've said from the start, that's what I say tonight.

So what does that mean? In short, it means amnesty for illegal aliens. Keep in mind, amnesty in this sense does not require a presidential pardon, and I found no evidence that would suggest President Obama has plans to grant any. He has on numerous occasions said his idea of immigration reform would consist of various stages ultimately designed to create a *path to citizenship* through compliance with certain conditions. Make no mistake, however; once you boil his plan down, what's left is a form of amnesty. President Obama is not the first president to push for immigration reform. I will explain the significance of this later.

If you read the wording carefully, you will find there were provisions in most of the versions of the proposed health-care reform bills that allowed coverage to immigrants who are here legally. Once the final draft of the legislation passed and amnesty is granted to illegal aliens via the *comprehensive immigration reform* legislation, they will no longer have illegal status and would therefore be eligible for benefits under the new health-care law. Some readers may claim I am taking liberties on what the president said. To them, I offer the following for consideration.

In February 2009, the DHS conducted a raid at Yamato Engine Specialists in Washington State, which resulted in the arrests of twenty-eight people suspected of being illegal aliens. This was the first work-site action since Janet Napolitano took charge of the department. According to an article published by the *New York Times*, the following day, Secretary Napolitano was not pleased about the raid—a raid that was conducted by her own department:[50]

> *A high-level official in the Department of Homeland Security said that Ms. Napolitano had not been informed about the raid on Tuesday before it happened, and that she was seeking details about its planning and scope, "She was not happy about it because it's inconsistent with her position, and the president's position on these matters." said the official, who agreed to discuss the matter on condition of anonymity because the secretary had not authorized the conversation.*

Some may say this was simply an example of a department head wanting to stay informed about the day-to-day operations of her department, as she should. That is a fair and valid point. To be equally fair, we must take a closer look at the other things Secretary Napolitano and the president have said "on these matters" to find the truth.

Both President Obama and Secretary Napolitano have claimed to support law enforcement measures that focus less on illegal workers and more on the employers who hire them. Again, if illegal aliens are granted amnesty, law enforcement measures on employers would become moot. In other words, if illegal aliens suddenly become legal aliens and eventually citizens, it is no longer illegal to hire them and there would be less *focus* on new illegal aliens who enter this country looking for the same status.

In addition, Secretary Napolitano apparently does not believe that being in the United States illegally is a crime to begin with. In an interview conducted by John King on CNN's *State of The Union,* she said,[51]

> *And yes, when we find illegal workers, yes, appropriate action, some of which is criminal, most of that is civil, because crossing the border is not a crime per se. It is civil.*

Pursuant to Title 8 USC Section 1325, crossing the border illegally is a crime. If you read only the code as originally written, it does appear to be only a civil matter. According to a 1990 amendment to the federal statute, however, it is considered a misdemeanor for the first offense and a felony for the second and subsequent offenses.

In another article published in August 2009, the *New York Times* reported,[52]

> *Ms. Napolitano and other administration officials have argued that a tough stance on illegal immigration is necessary to convince American voters to accept a wider overhaul that would give legal status to millions of foreigners.*

Is this an example of a shell game, or is it a mind game? Actually, it is both. After hearing their boss speak of cracking down on the problem of illegal immigration, immigration and customs enforcement agents went to work. They began conducting investigations and raids on several workplaces across the United States with amazing success.

It would appear they failed to understand Secretary Napolitano who probably did not really mean what she was saying; it was only political rhetoric which was *necessary to convince American voters to accept a wider overhaul that would give legal status to millions of foreigners.* (emphasis mine)

Perhaps it is because of my family ties, but the thought which immediately came to mind when I first read this was how close this approach is to the brainwashing techniques used by some of the FLDS leaders: set them up with one thing; when you have them where you want them, slap them with your true agenda.

In March 2009, Napolitano decided to delay a series of immigration raids and other workplace actions aimed at finding illegal workers. Apparently, that "tough stance" is nothing more than an attempt to lull conservatives into a false sense of security while the end game is to achieve the goals of the politically correct left.

One of the many tactics used by those who use political correctness to achieve their agenda-driven goals is to take advantage of the natural human instinct of compassion for others. They attempt to tug at the heartstrings of people by exaggerating the severity of problems in order to gain support for their cause. To illustrate this point, I offer the following two examples.

Speaker of the House of Representatives, Nancy Pelosi, while speaking about illegal immigration law enforcement efforts to a crowd at St. Anthony's Church in San Francisco, said,[53]

> *Who in this country would not want to change a policy of kicking in doors in the middle of the night and sending a parent away from their families? It must be stopped . . . What value system is that? I think it's*

un-American. I think it's un-American. We have to have
a change in policy and practice and again . . . I can't say
enough, the raids must end. The raids must end.

These comments were made before a mostly Hispanic crowd, which some say also contained illegal aliens. She went on to say,

You are special people. You're here on a Saturday night
to take responsibility for our country's future. That makes
you very, very patriotic.

This is a classic example of politically correct rhetoric. While the scenario Speaker Pelosi describes probably does occur, I do *not* believe it occurs at the level she suggests. If it did, I imagine it would be the lead story of almost every major news agency on a regular basis.

A large number of raids carried out by ICE are on job sites. Do ICE agents enter private homes to seek out illegal aliens? When they receive tips from concerned citizens, or through other means and are given reasons to believe private homes are harboring illegal aliens, they do investigate. If enough evidence is found during the course of those investigations to warrant such action, they do enter those homes. This is, of course, one of the duties assigned to an immigration *enforcement* agency; but they do it legally. That is when they are allowed to do it at all.

While I have found no evidence abuses have occurred, the laws of logic and probability dictate that there probably have been some cases where ICE agents have overreacted in the way they have conducted these raids at job sites and homes. Even if this has occurred, we should not condemn the entire police force for a few bad cops.

In my second example, then candidate Obama spoke to the National Council of La Raza, a pro immigration organization, about the same topic and said,[54]

When communities are terrorized by ICE immigration
raids, when nursing mothers are torn from their babies,
when children come home from school to find their parents

missing, when people are detained without access to legal
counsel, when all that is happening, the system just isn't
working, and we need to change it.

Here is yet another example of a politically correct politician attempting to take advantage of instinctive human compassion, not only to get elected but also to further a political agenda as well.

Are communities really being *terrorized* by ICE? Well, if I were someone who entered this country illegally, who obtained falsified documents attempting to cover up that crime, possibly engaging in identity theft during the course of obtaining those documents, was a part of a very large group of people contributing to the problem of overcrowding our public schools and health-care institutions mostly free of charge, perhaps I would consider myself to be terrorized by the efforts of law enforcement to bring me to justice. Or would the *terror* I felt simply be my desire to avoid getting caught for violating the law?

Again, I believe the desire of the overwhelming majority of illegal aliens is to provide a better way of life for themselves and their families, but we should keep in mind, all actions have consequences. If you break the law, be prepared for the consequences of your actions. But when you get caught breaking the law, don't blame someone else for your actions.

If it's fair to say illegal aliens feel terrorized by efforts of law enforcement, isn't it also fair to say executives at Enron felt terrorized by the efforts of state and federal agencies investigating their crimes? After all, those executives were also trying to make a better life for themselves and their families by becoming even wealthier. Okay, that last statement was sarcasm on my part.

But is there really *that* much difference between the two? In the case of Enron, corporate executives cheated investors out of billions of dollars to serve their own personal needs. Illegal aliens are collectively cheating taxpayers—and those whose identities they have illegally taken—out of billions of dollars, also for their own personal needs. Obviously, the main difference is in the two groups' intentions. Unlike Enron corporate executives, I do not believe most illegal aliens *intentionally desire* to cheat anyone. While I certainly have a high level of compassion for the plight of illegal aliens and virtually none for fat-cat corporate executives of Enron, I cannot ignore the fact that the end result is the same: innocent people (investors and/ or taxpayers) are being cheated.

The second part of Obama's statement, "when nursing mothers are torn from their babies," disturbed me, as I am sure it would most people. After all, who would *not* want to change a policy that condones tearing nursing mothers from their babies?

But did this actually happen? To answer that question I searched the Internet for articles addressing the issue. Although I did not find evidence of any nursing mother actually being "torn" from her baby by law enforcement agents, I did find a 2007 *New York Times* article written by Julia Preston, which said,[55]

> *Federal immigration agents were searching a house in Ohio last month when they found a young Honduran woman nursing her baby.*
>
> *The woman, Saída Umanzor, is an illegal immigrant and was taken to jail to await deportation. Her 9-month-old daughter, Brittney Bejarano, who was born in the United States and is a citizen, was put in the care of social workers.*
>
> *The decision to separate a mother from her breast-feeding child drew strong denunciations from Hispanic and women's health groups. Last week, the Immigration and Customs Enforcement agency rushed to issue new guidelines on the detention of nursing mothers, allowing them to be released unless they pose a national security risk.*

Even though the article was entitled, "Immigration Quandary: A Mother Torn From Her Baby," it did not claim ICE agents physically separated Saida and Brittney while she was actually breastfeeding her baby; nor did it cite examples of any other nursing mothers being "torn" from their babies in this way. It did speak of the problem of nursing mothers being held in detention facilities and not allowed access to their babies in order to breastfeed them.

Apparently, the agency took the necessary steps to correct this and other related problems, as the article goes on to explain,

> *Yesterday, Immigration and Customs Enforcement released new written guidelines for agents, establishing how they should treat single parents, pregnant women, nursing mothers and other immigrants with special child or family care responsibilities who are arrested in raids.*

Those corrections were made in 2007—the year before Obama gave his speech. Even if I misinterpreted what this article said, and the ICE agents did physically remove the baby from her mother's breast, the problem had already been dealt with, which made Obama's statement unnecessary and misleading.

It is not my intention to criticize the *New York Times* reporter's choice of words used in the title. In the article itself, Preston did appear to tell what actually happened according to the information she was given. The wording of her title (although some may consider it to be PC) is sometimes referred to as an attention getter designed to entice readers to the article. The more articles people read in a newspaper, the more likely they are to buy the next issue, which translates into more newspapers being sold. When politicians use these tactics, they are trying to sell something as well.

During the course of my research on Obama's speech, I read an anonymous blog post on a website called *Rhetoric Wars* that criticized Michelle Malkin and Ed Morrissey who wrote unfavorably of Obama's remarks in their respective websites. The anonymous author attempted to defend (or perhaps justify) what Obama said by pointing out the apparent lack of understanding on the part of Malkin and Morrissey as to the exact grammar Obama used. The *Rhetoric Wars'* author chose the following quote from Malkin's article:[56]

> *As for President-elect Obama, his true views about ICE are well-known. Despite telling Katie Couric that his aunt should be required to follow the law because "We're a nation of laws . . . I'm a strong believer you have to obey the law," Obama scolded ICE agents who do their jobs for "terrorizing" communities.*

And the following is *Rhetoric Wars'* point:

> *If you answered that the conjunction "despite" should indicate not just contrast but some sort of connection or contingency that was contradicted (e.g. "Despite her liberal views, she voted for the conservative candidate"), you saw through Malkin's rhetorically abusive strategy. There is of course no connection (and not even a contradiction) between Obama's belief that his aunt should obey the law in a nation of laws, and his rebuke of ICE agents for terrorizing communities. Criticizing police brutality is not the same as criticizing all police or the laws they enforce.*

The Hot Air [Morrissey] *article that Malkin links to makes the same sort of erroneous generalization (if Obama criticizes certain enforcers, he criticizes all enforcement), and uses equivocation as well to besmirch the candidate.*

Using the author's own logic, is it fair to say Malkin actually made an erroneous generalization as claimed? By saying Obama scolded ICE agents *who do their jobs* for terrorizing communities, is she referring to *all* ICE agents? Or is she instead referring to only those who have been accused of police brutality by him? I could argue that Obama stating his belief that his aunt (and everyone else) should obey the laws of this nation while criticizing even *certain enforcers* is a contradiction. ICE agents and other law enforcement agents are required by law to enforce the laws of our nation that are currently in place—even though some law enforcement officers (and politicians) may believe to be unjust.

The *Rhetoric Wars* author then quotes Morrissey's comment made on the *Hot Air* (Morrissey) website:

> So now the US government is a terrorist organization? Not only does this demonstrate his demagoguery on immigration, it also shows his cluelessness in the war on terrorists. If he can't tell the difference between al-Qaeda and ICE, then not only should he not be President, but Illinois needs to answer for his selection as a Senator.

The following is the anonymous author's response:

> True enough, Obama used the verb "terrorize". But does that mean he considers the ICE agents "terrorists"? If I say "As a child, Ted was terrorized by playground bullies," am I somehow linking Ted's persecutors with Osama Bin Laden? When Obama says "the system just isn't working, and we need to change it," is he saying we need to eliminate the system, or simply that we need to reform the enforcement so that nursing mothers aren't snatched from babies, detainees are provided with counsel, etc."

Does someone need to remind the *Rhetoric Wars* author and Obama again that policy within ICE has already been changed to correct problems in this area?

It is clear to me (and probably almost everyone else who read the post) Morrissey is speaking metaphorically. I doubt if he actually believes Obama sees the United States government as a terrorist organization, or that each citizen of Illinois should literally be required to explain why they elected Obama to the Senate. It is called exaggerating to make a point.

Some may argue Pelosi and Obama were doing the same thing with their comments: exaggerating to make a point. They would be correct. They could also argue that Pelosi and Obama have just as much right to use this method to make their points as Malkin,

Morrissey, the *Rhetoric Wars* blog author, and I do. Again, they would be correct.

The difference in this situation is the four of us can voice our opinions all we wish, but we do not have the legislative or executive power to actually change laws or official government policy. Speaker Pelosi does, and then senator Obama did. As president, Obama now has even greater power. Don't you think people with that much power should be more accurate and honest when speaking about problems in this country?

The anonymous author ends the post with the following cautionary and fair warning:

> *Watch out for what looks like lazy language. In the hands of propagandists, it's really an attempt to indoctrinate lazy readers.*

The author was referring to people like Malkin and Morrissey, but we should also heed the same advice when we read the words of politicians—perhaps more so. We should also not be fooled by attempts by some to defend politicians who will say whatever it takes to get elected whether what they say is true or not.

Some radical liberals like to think of themselves as well-educated, open-minded *progressive thinkers* whose duty it is to *educate and inform* those they see as inferior or ignorant. They take such arrogant, self-serving attitudes so far as to claim they are advancing their cause by engaging in, and winning (if only in their minds) what some of them refer to as *intellectual combat* with those who have opposing views.

These *intellectual warriors* attempt to keep their opponents off balance by employing a *daze and confuse* strategy—another shell game tactic. If someone makes a valid point, they counter with an alternative point designed to force their opponent to pause and consider, then throw in another point for them to contemplate before they can figure out the first one was only a decoy. By the time the opponent figures out what has happened, the battle is over. The warrior claims victory and walks away, or the opponent, realizing it is useless to debate someone who is only interested in playing games, becomes frustrated and wisely retreats. The warrior considers the latter their ultimate victory.

One day I happened to come upon a debate between one of these warriors and his opponent. Even though I disagreed with the warrior's position, I decided to stay out of the debate and observe the interactions between the two. At its conclusion, the opponent threw up his hands, walked away mumbling something about not being able to reason with an unreasonable man. The warrior chuckled as he watched his opponent leave.

After his opponent was out of earshot, I asked the warrior if he truly believed what he had said during the debate. He answered, "Of course not. His [opponent's] arguments were sound and his points were valid. I actually agree with him on everything he said." So I asked him the obvious question: "If you knew he was speaking the truth, why did you so adamantly oppose him?" If I live to be a hundred years old, I will never forget his response: "The truth has nothing to do with it. It is all about winning the battle which proves, unlike my opponent, I am an intellectual."

I had to remind the warrior that he did not change the mind of his opponent who even he admitted was correct all along. I also reminded him the actual purpose of having a debate was for two or more people with opposing views to state their views, argue the pros and cons of their positions, and through reason and logic, determine the truth, and find a workable solution to the problem at hand.

Attempting to draw me into a debate, he immediately suggested that he had played the role of devil's advocate by expressing opinions that differed from conventional thinking, and by doing so, he could possibly help determine the real truth. I responded by telling him I had no problem with that approach provided he was legitimately seeking the truth instead merely winning some silly battle.

I also pointed out the opinions of all three of us, although interesting, become irrelevant without merit. They are still only opinions. At the end of the day, the truth is still the truth whether we accept it as truth or not. Realizing he had already admitted his tactics and objective to me, the warrior walked away.

It was for that reason I believe the warrior lost the debate. Not because he walked away, but because he knew the opinions he gave were without merit. He also knew that I knew it.

These warriors may be well-educated, and may even have a higher IQ than you, but don't be intimidated by this. An intelligent person can take a large heap of cow manure, cover it up with tarps, dress it up with flower arrangements and sculptures, and call it art. But the truth is, once you get down to the bottom of it, it is still just a huge pile of crap.

Take the time to research their claims, think about what they said, the way they said it, and why they said it. With a little common sense, you can make a truly intelligent and informed decision whether or not that person is presenting a fair and valid point or just another pile of crap. I also advise caution in this endeavor. Don't allow your preconceived notions of a particular subject to cloud your judgment.

Another tactic of an intellectual warrior is to challenge their opponent's level of intelligence, thereby attempting to discredit not only their opponents but also their opponent's views as well. If they can successfully accomplish this goal, others will hesitate to challenge the warrior's views in fear of suffering the same fate.

In an episode first aired on August 24, 2009, comedian and political satirist Bill Maher made a guest appearance on *The Tonight Show* with Conan O'Brian. During the interview, O'Brian asked Maher to comment on remarks Maher had made earlier where he claimed, "America is stupid." Maher pointed out polls that show (according to Maher) 10 percent of Americans don't know Hawaii is a state, among other things. Later in the show, Maher expressed his views on how President Obama should proceed with the debate over the then-proposed health-care reform legislation.

I first heard about Maher's *Tonight Show* interview while watching *The Glen Beck Program* on Fox News Channel. The following is from the transcript of the video portion of Maher's *Tonight Show* interview aired on Beck's show:[57]

> *But yeah, I mean, they are talking about sixty votes.*
> *Forget this stuff, sixty. We can't get Americans to agree on*
> *anything 60 percent. Sixty percent of people don't believe*
> *in evolution in this country. He* [Obama] *just needs to*
> *drag them to it. Like I just said, they're stupid. Just drag*
> *them to this. Get healthcare done.*

The moment I saw the video, my first thought about the way Beck presented what Maher said was that Maher's comments could have been taken out of context. And exactly who was Maher referring to? So I looked up the video of the entire interview online to find out for myself. I discovered, the people whom Maher was referring to were not only the American people in general but also members of Congress as well. Maher even suggested how Obama should deal with one of the congressional panels assigned to create the health-care bill:[58]

> *You know, with or without them, make the gang of six an*
> *offer they can't refuse. This Max Baucus guy, he needs to*
> *wake up tomorrow with an intern's head in his bed.*

Maher also claims Obama should adopt what he suggests was the attitude of former president George W. Bush:[59]

> *I'm just gonna get it through. Suck on it, America, if*
> *you don't like it.*

He goes on to say that Obama should explain to the American public that the reason we have a two trillion dollar health-care reform bill is because Americans eat poorly. Maher even offers to teach O'Brian how to eat, to which O'Brian sarcastically replies, "What is that?"

Maher said that Republicans think Obama is a Socialist and suggests America needs a third political party:[60]

And they think Obama is a Socialist. Socialist? He's not even a Liberal. What we need is a Progressive Party in this country and we don't have it.

There is that *progressive* word again. Is Maher suggesting we need progressive thinkers in a new political party? That sounds great! After all, who wouldn't want a political party comprised of people who think progressively? That is, unless if by *Progressive Party* he means a new political party whose platform is, *"Live and Let Live! Unless you are not living exactly the way we say you should. And if you're not, we'll drag you to it, cram it down your throat, and you can just suck on it, America!"* In that case, no, thanks, I'll pass.

I believe we have entirely too much of that attitude in Washington DC now. This country is supposed to be governed by the will of the people, not the few. If I recall correctly, Bill Maher didn't much care for the things George W. crammed down his and everybody else's throat.

Which brings me to another point: if politicians would spend more time listening to and following the true will of the people there would be no reason for them to cram anything down the throats of the American people. While it is true that many Americans can't even find Hawaii on a map let alone know that it is a state, most Americans know what they want and don't want from our government.

Some people say that Bill Maher should not be allowed to make these kinds of comments because they are "un-American." I couldn't disagree more. Every American has the right to say what they think even if I or anyone else disagrees with them, or if someone believes what is said is un-American. If you don't like what Maher has to say, present an opposing view—as I have done—or simply change the channel.

Maher and I have very little common ground on our respective beliefs, but whether I agree with him or not, I do respect the fact that the opinions he states appear to be his own and not propaganda spoon-fed to him by others. I think Glen Beck said it best during his radio show:[61]

Bill Maher, I disagree with almost everything that spills out of this man's mouth but I appreciate the fact that he at least says what he means and means what he says. You know who Bill Maher is. That's a good thing. This is the kind of person that you can actually have an honest conversation with because I mean, he will throw bombs and everything else, but at least you can have an honest conversation because he's not hiding behind some sort of political correctness and some persona that is all warm and fuzzy when indeed he's a mountain lion behind it.

Other celebrities, although on the surface appear to be saying what they mean, seem to take a more Saul Alinsky style *the ends justify the means* approach by discrediting their opponents at all cost to further a hidden agenda.

Janeane Garofalo (actor, activist) made a guest appearance on MSNBC's *Countdown* hosted by Keith Olbermann in April 2009. Olbermann opened this segment of the show by criticizing people who attended the so-called Tea Party rallies across the country the day before. He was also critical of what he called their corporate sponsors. He showed a video clip of an unemployed blogger named Jeff who spoke at a Florida Tea Party rally and said,[62]

I want to start off by honoring the service of our veterans, our current service members, [something inaudible about parents] thank you so much for all you've done for this country. I also want to say, a little history lesson here. Back in 2000, there was a budget surplus in the country. And then the next ten years, it was destroyed by the profligate spending by the Bush administration. Here we are today in a situation where we have to . . . Cheer if you make less than $250,000 in a year. Just cheer. Your taxes are going to be cut under the current budget. Congratulations.

I was laid off in September because my employer had to make budget cuts. That was before the election. Let's remember if you're going to argue about more taxes and less spending, to place the blame where the blame belongs and that's squarely in the hands of the Republican congress and . . . [last part of speech inaudible due to crowd reaction]

Due to the poor quality of the audio portion and the background noise of the above-mentioned video, it is possible I may have misquoted a word or two spoken by Jeff. Given those conditions, I believe it is as accurate as possible. If not, I do apologize not only to Jeff but also to you the reader as well.

At the conclusion of the video, Olbermann said,

Congratulations, Pensacola tea baggers. You got spunked.

Olbermann later introduced Garofalo who said,

Thank you. You know, there's nothing more interesting than seeing a bunch of racists become confused and angry at a speech they're not quite certain what he's saying. It sounds right and then it doesn't make sense. Which, let's be very honest about what this is about. It's not about bashing Democrats, it's not about taxes, they have no idea what the Boston Tea Party was about, they don't know their history at all. This is about hating a black man in the White House. This is racism straight up. That is nothing but a bunch of tea bagging rednecks. And there is no way around that.

And you know, you can tell these types of right-wingers anything and they'll believe it, except the truth. You tell them the truth and they become—it's like showing Frankenstein's monster fire. They become confused, and angry and highly volatile.

That guy, causing them feelings they don't know, because their limbic brain, we've discussed this before, the limbic brain inside a right-winger or Republican or conservative or your average white power activist, the limbic brain is much larger in their head space than in a reasonable person, and it's pushing against the frontal lobe. So their synapses are misfiring.

Is Bernie Goldberg listening? Because Bernie might not have heard this when I said this the first time. So, Bernie, this is for you. It is a neurological problem we're dealing with.

During the course of this rant, Olbermann appears to agree with her statements then asks these questions:

Well, what do we do about it, though? I mean, our friend in Pensacola there who played them like a $3 fiddle and led them right down the garden path with nothing but facts and then they went, "Wait a minute, that doesn't sound like Rush Limbaugh." If you can't get them to make that last leap to what are we all doing here, Howard Johnson is wrong, how do you break through that?

Garofalo replies,

I don't think you do, for most of them. This is a—it's almost pathological or elevated to a philosophy or lifestyle. And again, this is about racism. It could be any issue, any port in the storm. These guys hate that a black guy is in the White House.

But they immigrant bash, they pretend taxes and tea bags, and like I said, most of them probably couldn't tell you thing one about taxation without representation, the Boston Tea Party, the British imperialism, whatever the history lesson has to be. But these people, all white for the most part, unless there's some people with Stockholm syndrome there.

Growing up in the South during the sixties and seventies, I heard a great deal of the racist, stereotypical, self-agenda-promoting propaganda of the group known as the Ku Klux Klan. Their members and other like-minded people attempted to spread their doctrine of hate to anyone within earshot. Though I never attended any KKK functions, I did hear them speak of how they believed black people to be *mongrels of society* and *subhumans who were genetically inferior to whites.* They also claimed that black people were unclean, riddled with disease and genetic defects, and were therefore intellectually inferior to whites. Because of all these inferiorities, those of the KKK mind-set believed that it was the responsibility of the white race to, wherever possible, *educate* these people as to their proper role in society with the exception of the few *good Negros*, of course. Sound familiar?

Just as I do, Maher, Olbermann, Garofalo, and others have every right to express their opinions. While I do admire people who call it as they see it, I do not admire or agree with people who resort to racially derogatory tactics to make their points, even when they use those tactics against members of their own race.

Contrary to popular belief, stereotypical and derogatory remarks made against one's own race are just as racist as those made about a different race. If you doubt this, just ask a black person born and raised in America who has been referred to as high yellow or has been called a porch Negro or an Uncle Tom by people of their own race.

A wise man once told me that political correctness is for those who cannot handle the reality of truth. I find that statement to be very true. I have no doubt that some of the people in the Tea Party crowds were there for the wrong reasons. And yes, judging strictly from the nature of some of their signs, a few—very few—were more than likely racists.

Growing up when and where I did and witnessing firsthand the things I have, I know racism when I see it. I can say this with 100 percent certainty because at one point in my life, I once was a racist.

But I wasn't born a racist, I was taught to be one. I repeated all the stereotypical rhetoric of the white racists who came before me as though it was normal and natural.

Fortunately for me, as I entered into my early teens, I began to realize that something wasn't right in this area. I knew that if I were to ever figure out the truth, I had to remove myself from my racist attitudes and observe people as they truly were. I began to pay closer attention to the racist claims and actions of those from both sides of the racial divide. Although it took me a couple of years to figure it out, I finally came to the conclusion that people of all colors are just that: people.

We may look different, but we all basically have the same dreams, hopes, desires, and fears. It is through those fears that we allow ourselves to become and act like people we shouldn't be. Once there, racism becomes a cycle of hate, which is difficult to break. It is not easy for a racist to hide or suppress their prejudices. It is even harder to break the cycle of hate. But even when you do, you never forget how you thought, which makes it easier to recognize it in others. Because I was once one myself, I know what racists think, I know how racists think, and I know how they act.

From what I have seen of the Tea Party protesters—some of which I have actually spoken with—and what they had to say, I feel confident that the overwhelming majority are not concerned about differences in skin color, but are instead concerned about the tendency of our leaders to get too involved in our personal and private lives, while at the same time driving our national debt to record levels through reckless spending.

After all, wasn't it the governmental reckless spending on the part of the Republican congress one of the things Jeff complained about? If it was so evil for the Republicans to do it—and I agree it was—why then is it suddenly acceptable when the Democrats do the exact same thing? Could it be because of the politically correct spin they place on their enormously expensive programs while attempting to distract us from them by calling the Tea Party members racists? Always remember Alinsky's "Rules for Radicals" concept of divide and conquer to distract from the main objective.

If the Tea Party members are as racist and simpleminded as Garofalo and Olberman suggested they would be very open about it just like the Klan was and still is. They simply would not have had the mental capacity or desire to avoid it. Instead of displaying racist behavior, the Tea Party movement has gone to great lengths to discourage and weed out the fringe racist element that inevitably infiltrates every organization of their size. Come to think of it, I wouldn't at all be surprised to find a racist or two working for MSNBC. And if that turned out to be true, does that mean MSNBC is a racist network?

It is a dangerous practice to use the race card too often. Just as with a credit card, if used too often, the race cardholder eventually uses all their credit—or in this case, their credibility. If this continues to happen, just as with the boy who cried wolf, people will soon start ignoring the cries of racism when legitimate racist activities do occur. And those who have overused the race card will have been the cause. Don't allow yourself to be conned by those who play the racist shell game to distract you from the real issues at hand.

People who made less than $250,000 in 2009 may or may not have their taxes cut depending on their circumstances. That is why each of us must submit an individual income tax return instead of being sent a bill by the government. It's easy to say our taxes will be cut, but that doesn't necessarily mean it will actually happen.

Even if they are cut for the majority of people, I'll also offer this for your consideration: with the excise taxes, fines and penalties included in the new health-care reform law, if those costs to the taxpayer become greater than the cuts from the current budget, at the end of the year are we really paying less in taxes overall? If we do wind up paying more taxes overall, then it will be the American people who have been played like a $3 fiddle and led right down the garden path only to get "spunked" (or did he mean punked?) by PC rhetoric. In fairness, perhaps in the heat of the moment, Jeff simply forgot to mention those facts.

I believe the leaders of this nation should be held to a higher standard than others—not necessarily legally, but certainly ethically. When politicians grossly exaggerate problems which may or may not exist, they are doing nothing more than using politically correct rhetoric and propaganda to further their own agenda, and usually their political party's agenda as well.

I would love to see the leaders of our country say what they mean and mean what they say. If they did, although we may not agree with everything they say, at least we would know where they truly stand, which helps us clarify where we stand. Unfortunately, for the American people, this will probably never happen. And if it doesn't, it will be because the politicians in our nation's capital (and elsewhere) are still too busy pulling tarps over huge piles of crap. If we sit by without speaking our minds in protest, we will continue to allow them to get by with calling it art.

CHAPTER EIGHT

One Vote, One Voice

When even one American—who has done nothing wrong—is forced by fear to shut his mind and close his mouth, then all of Americans are in peril.

—Harry S. Truman

Always vote for principle, though you may vote alone, and you may cherish the sweetest reflection that your vote is never lost.

—John Quincy Adams

Midway through the process of writing this book, I was talking to a friend of mine about not realizing just how difficult writing it would be. I wasn't referring to the long hours of research I needed to do, or time spent at my computer actually writing, or battling through the occasional bouts of writer's block. I expected those things to be difficult, time-consuming, and at times, frustrating. I was referring to the challenge of exactly how to get my points across while being as fair, honest, and compassionate as possible, and at the same time doing so without using PC. That, as you might imagine, is not an easy task.

Some may say I have done an excellent job of achieving my goal while others may point out places where I have failed. Fair enough. I would be the first to be surprised to learn that I had made it entirely through this process without using some form of PC. But even if I have, it only goes further to prove my point; our society has been systematically brainwashed by the use of political correctness in almost every facet of our lives. How could I not include myself in that claim?

Upon hearing about my dilemma, my friend suggested I tell the reader just how difficult writing about this subject was, and why. After some consideration, I have chosen to take that advice. I will also offer a few suggestions on how to correct some of the problems I've brought up already and a few I haven't.

Just like everyone else, I have been bombarded with PC phrases and attitudes on a daily basis. I have been exposed to it through the news media, advertising and marketing, political discussions, philosophers, literature and art just to name a few. I have always found it annoying, misleading, and in most cases downright untrue. But it was not until recent years that I began to realize just how dangerous it really is.

When I first sat down to write, I had preconceived ideas of how things are in this world and why. So, feeling confident that I knew what I was talking about, I began writing pages of material stating my views, even before doing research. Perhaps that was a flawed method, but I found that I was exposing myself to just how much I had been influenced by a lifetime of political correctness.

As I began doing research to back up my claims, I realized that some of those claims were not based entirely on facts and others were just plain wrong. I then realized that those flawed beliefs were based (to a surprisingly large degree) on the subliminal messaging of PC. That certainly changed my views on those topics, and I subsequently made the appropriate revisions.

So there I was, a man opposed to political correctness most of my life and confident about my stance on the subject. And even though I made every attempt to guard myself against PC, I realized I had not protected myself sufficiently.

I fully understand the possibility that the views and opinions I express here may not be completely accurate according to the true facts. It is important to remember, research material is only as accurate as the provider. People are sometimes misquoted or have their statements taken out of context. Recorded materials are sometimes edited or otherwise altered. It is always best to obtain information whenever possible straight from the source, and then check other sources to confirm its accuracy.

With that in mind, I do believe everything I say here to be the truth based on the research material I have found along with my personal assessment of it. I also understand that if credible evidence were to surface to disprove something I have stated that it is my responsibility to properly reevaluate my views based on that evidence.

Political correctness has become a brainwashing technique used to reassign our subconscious thought. It has become so embedded into our society that it has caused most Americans to fail to openly and publicly speak their minds about things they believe to be problems in this country because they fear retribution from those who either promote or buy into the tactics of PC. They see what happens to those who do find the courage to speak out against PC's sacred cows. For an example of this, we need only look at current events.

In the first several months of his term in office, President Obama has been criticized for nearly every one of his policies. This is nothing new. Every president since George Washington has suffered exactly the same fate. Having good, honest, open, and productive public debates on issues is one of the ways we as a nation can ensure no one person or branch of government becomes too powerful and problems can be solved in a positive manner.

However, I have noticed in almost every case thus far, when someone disagrees with the policies of, or the statements made by President Obama or his administration, they are called racists simply because the President is black. It apparently makes no difference to the accusers if these critics have a valid point or not. Obama's critics are still accused of not only political bias but also racial bias as well. Are those who accuse others of being racists standing up against oppression? Or are they doing nothing more than using PC tactics in an attempt to discredit critics and divert attention away from what they have to say?

It is possible to disagree with someone of a different color without having their color be a factor. We should not allow this or any other PC tactic to derail our search for the truth.

Before I begin listing what I believe to be basic solutions that could solve many of the problems we face in this country, I want to discuss my political party affiliation. I have none. This may come as a surprise to those of you who have already dubbed me a conservative or a Republican based on what I have said so far. You may even believe

I am simply fooling myself into thinking I am not those things. If so, I suggest you pay close attention to what I am about to say and then read what I have already said again, this time paying closer attention.

I was born and raised in the South, which has been a traditionally conservative region, but I now live in California, which has been traditionally liberal. When I voice my political views in the South, I am accused of being a *bleeding heart liberal*. When I voice those same views in California, I am accused of being a *right-wing extremist*. Obviously, I can't be both. No matter what others may think, I support what I believe makes the most sense overall. I try to use common sense to make those determinations.

One thing I would suggest to others: if you find yourself so far away from political common sense that you consider yourself either right wing or left wing, perhaps you should reevaluate your views and how you obtained them. That doesn't mean you can't or shouldn't be a liberal or a conservative. It also doesn't mean you should be on the fence. But if you are so far away from that fence that you can't listen to what the other side is saying, how can you possibly ever hope to find a workable compromise? And if you are unwilling to compromise with the other side simply because they are the *other side*, please read the suggestion at the beginning of this paragraph again.

There have been times in our nation's history when we have achieved great successes and when we have experienced great failures. We must always remember that it was during the times when we put aside our petty differences and worked together for a common goal that we have been successful. It is those times when we haven't that we've failed.

As an example of the type of compromises I speak of, below are a few of my political beliefs:

I believe in *limited* social services such as social security, Medicare, Medicaid, and yes even welfare. I firmly believe we as Americans have a deep charitable desire to assist those among us who are truly unable to care for themselves, or are in need of temporary assistance to help them get back on their feet. I do not believe that responsibility extends to those who are guilty of committing widespread abuses of these programs.

Those who abuse the system are not only sucking it dry and placing a higher tax burden on the rest of us, but they are also stealing money, which could be used to pay higher benefits to those who truly need it, as well as making those systems more efficient, and ultimately stronger. When I think of the abuses of these and other social programs, I am reminded of something Dwight D. Eisenhower once said,

A people that values its privileges above its principles soon loses both.

I believe we need certain laws and regulations to prevent big business and others from obtaining too much control over us or from taking advantage of us. For example, I believe we need agencies like the Food and Drug Administration to prevent food companies from poisoning us. At the same time, I do not believe we should allow our government to tell us what we can and cannot eat or to impose higher taxes on the foods it deems unfit. I find it highly hypocritical when politicians who support abortion claim the government has no right to tell women what to do with their bodies, and then in the next breath tell us we are not allowed to eat certain types of food because of the effect those foods have on our bodies.

I believe in each of us paying our fair share of taxes to keep our government running. I do not believe in a government so big that taxpayers can't afford to pay what is necessary to keep it running. Nor do I believe we need to waste money by having more than one agency that does basically the same thing; one FDA is enough. If you can't figure out how to place all regulations pertaining to food and drugs under the control of one agency, you have no business being in government.

I believe in freedom of the press, but I also believe the press should be unbiased. Otherwise, it becomes nothing more than a propaganda (or PC) machine.

I believe no government has the right to establish a state or national religion or force any religious beliefs upon its citizens. Nor do I believe any government has the right to restrict a show of respect for the religious beliefs of its citizens just because they are a government entity or employed by one. I also believe in the right of citizens to have no religious beliefs at all. But I do not believe those without religious beliefs have the right to attempt to remove the rights of those who do—and vice versa—especially while claiming to be *protecting* the people or the Constitution in the process.

I believe in *limited* gun control. I agree with registration of certain types of weapons because doing so assists law enforcement in investigating violent crimes. I agree with having a *reasonable* waiting period between the purchase, and taking possession of a gun to prevent someone in a temporarily stressed frame of mind from doing something they would later regret.

However, I do not believe our government should have so much control over our weapons that the ability of our citizens to defend themselves becomes jeopardized. I do not believe the government has the right to require the registration of or restrict access to ammunition for normal weapons; that is nothing more than an end around method to prevent people from defending themselves. And in no way do I believe our government or anyone else has the right to disarm private citizens—through legislation or otherwise. In fact, doing so is against the laws of our Constitution.

It is absolutely vital to our national security that we maintain a strong national defense to protect ourselves against those who threaten our sovereignty from both foreign and domestic sources. Part of that strong national defense is the right for private citizens to keep and bear arms, which is protected by the Second Amendment of the Constitution.

It is no coincidence the right to keep and bear arms was placed so high on the list of amendments. If you read the first ten amendments to the Constitution (more commonly known as the Bill of Rights), you will gain insight into what our founding fathers considered to be the most important rights of the people.

Some gun control activists claim we would all be safer if the possession of guns by private citizens were to be made illegal. They believe we must rid our country of all privately owned guns to prevent accidental shootings involving children. Those accidents do occur, and they are indeed tragic. But those accidents can easily be prevented by the responsible and proper handling and storing of weapons in the home and elsewhere.

These activists also claim if the possession of guns were illegal, it would prevent their use in violent crimes. If the failure of Prohibition laws in the early twentieth century proved anything to us, it was this: when the government prohibits the American people from having something we truly desire, we will find a way to obtain it in spite of the law. Criminals are well aware of this fact; why aren't the activists?

If a person really wants to kill someone, they will find a way, with or without a gun. And if you happen to be the one that person means to kill, do you really want to be unarmed? A can of pepper spray or a black belt in karate won't work very well against a man with a gun twenty-five feet away. But if he knows or even thinks you also have a gun and you are willing to use it, he'll think twice before knocking down your door.

Another argument gun control activists often use to justify the disarmament of American citizens is, "Do deer hunters really need an AK-47 to shoot a deer?" Well, no.

> The Second Amendment to the U.S. Constitution states that a *well regulated Militia, being necessary to the security of a free State, the right of the people to keep and bear Arms, shall not be infringed.*" (emphasis mine)

Many of our founding fathers spoke often about the importance of a citizen's right to keep and bear arms. Thomas Jefferson said on the subject,

> *No man shall ever be debarred the use of arms. The strongest reason for the people to retain the right to keep and bear arms is, as a last resort, to protect themselves against tyranny in government.*

> *What country can preserve its liberties if its rulers are not warned from time to time that their people preserve the spirit of resistance? Let them take arms.*

George Washington said,

> *Firearms are second only to the Constitution in importance;*
> *they are the peoples' liberty's teeth.*

With these words in mind, and taking into account what these men went through to form this nation, do you really believe the gun control movement by some activists and politicians in this country is actually about what weapons deer hunters use?

While I don't believe the current political climate warrants an armed uprising of the people, those in power must be reminded at all times that the people hired them to represent the will of the people as a whole, not the will of a few. They must also be reminded that it was the people who put them in office and it is the people who can and will remove them if it becomes necessary. They should also remember that the people have the legal and Constitutional right to do so.

Our elected officials work for us, not the other way around. We hired them and we can fire them. We can remove them by way of recall or voting for someone else on election day or by placing so much pressure on them that they have no choice but to resign. Because of years of corruption and politically motivated maneuvering, politicians have the power to make whatever laws they deem fit. They also have the backing of politically partisan judges to put whatever spin necessary on the constitutionality of those laws in order to further their agendas.

Events such as the bombing of Pearl Harbor on December 7, 1941, and the terrorist attacks of September 11, 2001, have shown us that when necessary, the people of the United States can and will put aside our differences for a belief in a common cause.

Those attacks were committed by foreign forces who wished to threaten our sovereignty as a nation and to fundamentally change or eliminate entirely our American way of life. But threats to our nation do not always come from outside our boundaries; sometimes they come from within. With each passing day, more and more Americans are beginning to realize this truth. As we do, we are beginning to put aside the old notion that our government is protecting us; we are coming to terms with the reality that we need to protect ourselves from our government.

I hope and pray with all my heart the day never comes when the American people find it necessary to rise up in armed revolt to put down the tyranny of our own government, although sometimes I fear it may. It is far past time for our elected officials to return to the basic concept of our founding fathers—a concept that was echoed so eloquently by President Abraham Lincoln during his "Gettysburg Address" on November 19, 1863:

> *That this nation, under God, shall have a new birth of freedom—and that government: of the people, by the people, for the people, shall not perish from the Earth.*

As I said before, I don't believe we are at the point where violence is warranted. I also believe and strongly endorse the notion that we can return this nation to the values with which it was founded without violent means. But these are only things I believe to be true. One thing I know to be true is that the majority of Americans will take whatever steps necessary to ensure this great nation, and the freedoms we have held so dear shall never perish from the earth without one hell of a fight. The choice of how that fight is fought is for the people to decide. May God help and guide us to make the smart choice.

For this and many other reasons in mind, I will list a few of the basic changes I believe could put us back on the path of restoring and preserving the freedoms we hold so dear as well as prevent the next armed and violent revolution from ever taking place.

First recommendation: Abolish the electoral college system

The electoral college system is like having a hitching post for horses in front of every store. It was a good idea in its time, but one that the passage of time and our modern forms of transportation and communication have made obsolete.

It is erroneous to think that we the people elect our presidents and vice presidents. In the 2008 presidential election, 131,461,089 Americans voted in total. Barrack Obama received 69,499,428 (52.87 percent) of those votes and became president of the United States on January 20, 2009. Therefore you could say Obama was elected president by over 69 million Americans but you would be wrong.

In fact, he was elected president by only 365 Americans. Technically, of the 538 Americans who legally elect the President, he only needed the vote of 270 of them to put him in office. Now I don't know about you, but I have a major problem with that. Not because of who was elected, but because of the system itself.

When our founding fathers got together to write the Constitution, they faced a dilemma: how to fairly elect the president and vice president. They were faced with five options:

1. By way of the popular vote of the people
2. By way of a debate and vote in the U.S. Congress
3. By way of a vote of the state legislators
4. By way of a vote of the state governors
5. By way of a vote by *electors*—the electoral college system

The founding fathers were apprehensive about the direct popular vote option. Without national political parties, there was no structure by which to choose and limit the number of candidates. In addition, travel and communication was slow and difficult. A person who may be the best candidate for president could be very popular in one region while unknown in others. With each region producing their most popular candidates, the vote would be split between too many candidates. The end result would probably be a misrepresentation of the overall will of the nation.

They were equally apprehensive about the elections by Congress option. This option would rely on the members of Congress to properly assess the will of the people (usually without direct contact) and to vote accordingly instead of promoting their own political agendas. They had similar concerns about relying on the votes of state legislators and state governors. The compromise left us with the electoral college.

But what exactly is the electoral college system and who are its members? Instead of giving you the entire history of the process, let's take a look at what it is today.

The electoral college is the system by which a small group of people called electors are either elected by popular vote of the people or appointed by various means to officially elect the president and vice president of the United States of America. Each state and the District of Columbia (DC) is allowed to have a number of electors equal to the number of representatives in the House of Representatives, and one each for its two senators.

For example, Texas has a total of thirty-four congressional representatives in Congress, consisting of thirty-two in the House, and two in the Senate. Therefore, Texas is allowed thirty-four electors, whereas Vermont with one member in the House and two in the Senate is allowed to have three electors.

These electors promise or *pledge* to cast their votes according to the will of the people as voiced through the results of the popular vote of their respective states. But only twenty-six states and the District of Columbia have laws or regulations that require electors to cast their votes according to the overall majority of the popular vote of their people.

The electors of the remaining twenty-four are free to cast their votes as they see fit—all 257 of them. Although it is very rare, there have been cases where a few electors have not voted according to the will of the people of their states. Normally this would have little, if any, impact on the outcome of the election due to the fact that most presidential elections have not been that close. But could it have an impact on a presidential election whether it is close or not? Could the will of the people be cast aside by a couple of rogue votes by electors? Or even one? The answer to all these questions is yes, it could.

There are currently 538 electors selected during the course of each presidential election. A candidate needs a total of 269 votes to tie, and 270 to gain a majority of electoral college votes to win the election. So for the sake of argument, let's say in a future presidential election, the two front running candidates are Thomas Smith (Democrat) and Carl Jones (Republican).

After all the popular votes are counted, the two candidates are in an apparent tie with 269 electoral college votes each, in spite of the fact Smith won the popular vote by an eight million vote margin. Then in December, if all the electors vote the way they were supposed to, and that vote officially ends in a tie, the decision of who is to be elected falls upon the House of Representatives in Congress per the provisions of Article II and the Twelfth Amendment to the Constitution. But the electors must first officially vote to confirm a tie.

Let's say during that vote, an elector from Indiana, in spite of the fact Smith won the popular vote in that state, decides Jones would make a better president (or for *any other* reason) and casts his or her electoral college vote for Jones. Because he or she lives in a state without restrictions to vote for any particular candidate, it would be perfectly legal for that person to do so. And by doing so, Jones would have 270 electoral votes. By law, Carl Jones would have the minimum number of electoral college votes required to officially win the election, and would become the next president of the United States of America. There would be nothing anyone could legally do about it.

This scenario has never unfolded in this country—at least not yet. But given the ever changing political climate in the United States, I believe it is simply a matter of time before it does.

Five times in our nation's relatively short history, the president has been officially elected by means of congressional vote, and/or with a lack of popular vote:

Thomas Jefferson: 1801

Three years prior to the ratification of the Twelfth Amendment, Thomas Jefferson and his running mate Aaron Burr won the popular vote but did not obtain the minimum required electoral college vote to take office. As a result, the election fell to Congress in what was believed to be nothing more than a formality, much as most Americans believe the electoral college vote is today. But due to some political maneuvering by members of a lame duck Congress who threw their support behind Burr instead of Jefferson, it took thirty-six ballots before Jefferson obtained the minimum votes required to become president. But it could have gone either way. The Twelfth Amendment prevented this scenario from ever becoming an issue again.

John Quincy Adams: 1824

Andrew Jackson won the popular vote but failed to obtain the 131 electoral college votes needed at that time to become president. Again, the decision was left up to Congress where through similar political maneuvering, John Quincy Adams was elected president. This was the first time in our nation's history where a person who lost the popular vote became president, but certainly not the last.

Rutherford B. Hayes: 1876

In 1876, there were a total of 369 electoral votes available with 185 needed to win. Hayes lost the popular vote by a slim margin, but because he won in enough of the more populous states, he was able to obtain the 185 electoral college votes needed to win. Hayes became the first president to take office by way of electoral college vote that was in conflict with the popular vote.

Benjamin Harrison: 1888

In 1888, there were a total of 401 electoral votes available with 201 needed to win. Benjamin Harrison received 5,439,853 popular votes and won 233 electoral votes. Grover Cleveland won the popular vote with 5,540,309 votes, but won only 168 electoral votes. In spite of losing the popular vote by a mere 100,456 votes, Harrison still managed to obtain a whopping sixty-five vote advantage in electoral college votes and was elected president. As you can see by these figures, if a politician campaigns in the right states, while mostly ignoring the people of the others, he or she can still become president.

George W. Bush: 2000

In 2000, as is still true today, there were a total of 538 electoral votes available with 270 needed to win. This election has proved to be one of the most controversial presidential elections in our history. The race between George W. Bush and Al Gore continued for over a month after the polls closed on election day. The election results in Florida were initially so close that a series of recounts were conducted for weeks amid legal maneuvering by both sides.

The largest part of the controversy came from recounts conducted in four counties, which were considered to be strongly under Democratic control, and where the new ballots used there for the first time were claimed to be confusing by a number of voters. Many of the ballots, because they were improperly used and therefore deemed invalid, were discarded. In the end, Bush was announced to be the winner in Florida, and received its twenty-five electoral college votes. Those twenty-five votes gave Bush a total of 271, and Bush was elected president in spite of losing in the popular vote nationwide, even counting the disputed votes in Florida.

Although he did recuse himself from the recount process from the start, the governor of the State of Florida at the time was none other than George W. Bush's brother, John Ellis "Jeb" Bush. Another interesting side note, although it had no effect on the final outcome of the 2000 presidential election, in the final electoral college vote, one Gore elector from the District of Columbia abstained from voting.

Some Bush supporters claim the 2008 election is an argument for continuing the electoral college system. The people who hold the highest office in our country should be elected by the majority of its citizens. It should not be left to the sometimes unpredictable conclusion of a few electors, and certainly not to the political maneuverings of politicians. I wonder if those Bush supporters would have felt the same way if the situation had been reversed.

With the inventions and advancements of speedy air travel, television, radio, and the Internet, the concerns our founding fathers had over the popular vote option has long since passed. So, too, has the need for the electoral college system.

Second recommendation: Congressional redistricting reform

Many people in the United States are probably unaware our congressional districts change every ten years. Many cannot tell you which district they reside in, or even the name of their representative in Congress. Some Americans have lived in more than one congressional district during the course of their lives even though they have always lived in the same area.

So how does this happen? Not because they move, but because the congressional lines move. In and of itself, this is nothing to be concerned about. Net population growth is higher in some areas over others. People searching for work (among other reasons) do relocate to different parts of the country. But in recent decades, other reasons for the shift in congressional lines have developed. The most dramatic of these reasons is the incredible influx of noncitizens since the days of Ellis Island.

Every ten years, the U.S. Census Bureau conducts what amounts to a nationwide head count. Through various means, the Census Bureau attempts to determine how many people actually live in this country, whether they are citizens or not. While doing so, they also collect statistical data such as ethnic background or race, average household occupancy, percentage of different age groups, etc. But the main job of the Census Bureau is not only to determine how many people live in this country but also where they live. Once that information is determined, congressional district boundaries are drawn according to the sparseness or concentration of the overall population.

Congressional districts determine how many members of the House of Representatives each state gets. Each state is allowed two senators who represent the entire state regardless of its population size.

For example, California has the largest population of any state, and therefore has the largest number of congressional districts of any state (fifty-three). Most of those districts are in metropolitan areas such as Los Angeles and the San Francisco Bay Area, with eighteen congressional districts in Los Angeles County alone. Alaska is the largest state in area but has one of the lowest population densities of any state, and therefore has only one congressional district for the entire state.

But how much of an impact do noncitizens really have on congressional redistricting in the United States? More than you may think. What effect does this really have on how Congress looks politically over the next ten years until the next census? And how much importance do politicians place on attempting to control how Congress looks politically for decades to come? Again, more than you may think.

Steven A. Camarota, PhD, director of research at the Center for Immigration Studies, prepared testimony for the House Subcommittee on Federalism and the census on the impact noncitizens could have on the 2010 census. The following is the introduction of that testimony:[63]

> The United States is currently experiencing the largest sustained wave of immigration in its history, with 1.5 million legal and illegal immigrants settling in the country each year. The foreign born or immigrant population stood at over 31 million in the 2000 Census, and the total has grown to 36 million by the end of 2005. There is an unfortunate tendency to view this immigration one dimensionally. Some see immigrants only as workers, other see them as a potential voters, or only the fiscal problem they may create, still others see only possible terrorists.
>
> All of these perspectives capture some aspect of immigration. But immigrants are much more than this. Immigrants are not simply things, they are human beings. As a result, their presence in the United States has wide ranging economic, cultural, demographic, national security, and political effects on our country. Whether one thinks the effects of

immigration is on balance a net gain or a net loss to the country, the fact remains its impact is very broad and not confined to one area.

This hearing is going to discuss one of the most often overlooked, but nonetheless important, effects they have: on political representation. If you take nothing else away from my testimony, it should be that allowing in people, even as guest workers or just tolerating illegal immigration has broad ranging effects. These effects include such things as the redistribution of House seats.

For example, if we take the 11 million illegals already here and grant them temporary status, the Census in 2010 will still count them, and seats will still be apportioned to states based on their presence. On the other hand, if we enforce the law and make most illegals go home, this too will have apportionment consequences in 2010. In our discussion of immigration, therefore, we should not compartmentalize its various impacts; instead, we must recognize the broad implications of immigration on virtually every aspect of American life, including apportionment.

Dr. Camarota went on to explain the percentage of noncitizens had grown from 3.1 percent to 8.7 percent of the total U.S. population in the past twenty-five years. That doesn't seem like much, right? It doesn't until you calculate the redistricting effect such a small percentage can have on congressional seats according to what Dr. Camarota says later in his testimony:

Immigration has a significant effect on the distribution of seats in the U.S. House of Representatives for three reasons. First, seats are apportioned based on each state's total population relative to the rest of the country, including illegal aliens and other non-citizens. This, of course, is the issue at the center of Congresswoman Miller's proposal.

Second, Congress has chosen to allow in a large number
of legal immigrants and to tolerate wide spread illegal
immigration. After the 2000 Census, the average
Congressional district had roughly 650,000 people. Thus,
the more than 18 million non-citizens in the 2000 Census
were equal to nearly 29 Congressional seats.

The third reason is that non-citizens are not evenly
distributed throughout the country. In 2000, half of all
non-citizens lived in just three states and almost 70 percent
live in just six states. States with a large non-citizen
population will gain at the expense of states comprised
mostly of citizens.

In a report entitled, "Remaking the Political Landscape:
The Impact of Illegal and Legal Immigration on
Congressional Apportionment", published by the Center for
Immigration Studies in October of 2003, we calculated the
impact of non-citizens on the distribution of seats in the
House. Overall we found that the presence of non-citizens
caused a total of nine seats to change hands. Indiana,
Michigan, Mississippi, Oklahoma, Pennsylvania, and
Wisconsin each lost a seat that they had prior to the 2000
Census while Montana, Kentucky and Utah each failed
to gain a seat they otherwise would have gained, but for
the presence of non-citizens in other states. Of the nine
seats redistributed by non-citizens, 6 went to California,
while Texas, New York and Florida each gained a seat and
New York retained a seat it otherwise would have lost.
Analysis of this kind is very straightforward, involving a
simple calculation of the apportionment of seats to states
with non-citizens included and then without them. Other
researchers have come to the same conclusion.

He later cites one of the other researchers:

These results are the same as those obtained by Marta Tienda in her 2002 article in Demography entitled "Demography and the Social Contract", pages 587-616.

This testimony is dated December 6, 2005. There can be little doubt those numbers have increased a great deal since then. The only way to truly reform the way we reapportion our congressional districts is to change the way we conduct our census.

First we need to develop a better system by which we count the people who live here. Because those who represent us in Congress are elected only by American citizens, we must have an accurate count of who are citizens and who are not. What point is there to potentially have congressional districts where only 20 percent of the adults living in those districts can vote? And how fair is it to those states that lose seats in Congress even though their population of citizens has grown?

But as Dr. Camarota said, noncitizens are not mere numbers, they are people too. I believe we should count all people living in this country, whether they are legal or not. But for the purpose of congressional redistricting we should only count American citizens. Noncitizens should be counted only for statistical purposes. If the people of a particular district are mostly sympathetic to the plight of immigrants, they simply vote for the congressional candidate who shares their views. At least this way, all American citizens would have a fair and equal voice in how our country operates.

My first two suggestions go hand in hand, but therein lies the problem in bringing about reform. The Constitution is very clear on both the electoral college and the census. To make the changes, I recommend on either issue would require constitutional amendments, which by design is no small task.

An amendment first needs to be passed by Congress, and then ratified by a three-quarters majority of the states. Although the vast majority of the people I have spoken to are overwhelmingly in favor of abolishing the electoral college system, several attempts to push it through Congress have failed.

Third recommendation: True immigration reform

I stated earlier that I am in favor of getting rid of illegal aliens. I am also in favor of immigration reform. Surprising? Not really. I agree with the president on this topic, though only in principle. I also agree in principle with the occasional need for effective stimulus packages and limited bailouts (I call it assistance) to certain major industries when we as a nation can afford to do so along with certain requirements being met by the companies receiving assistance. I believe we need health care and health insurance reform. I also believe none of these things would be necessary if the leaders of our nation devoted more time to properly deal with issues that arise than devote their time to promote their political agendas.

If you are going to develop plans for such things, you must develop plans that will actually work without placing our nation's economy at further risk. As I said before, in order to solve any problem, we must first take a hard, honest look at the overall situation—the big picture—then find workable solutions based on that knowledge. I think this administration has failed to do so, but the Obama administration is not alone.

One of the places I have lived in California is a little town just north of the Mexican border. I have seen my fair share of people crossing the border illegally—not just Mexicans, but people from as far south as South America as well. About three years ago, a man who had walked (yes, walked!) from South America died due to dehydration after making it only a mile inside the United States.

On more than one occasion, I have had to swerve my car to avoid small groups of people running across the freeway on my way to work. Although I have not heard of any of these people being hit by cars, I have heard of cases where cars have run off the freeway trying to avoid them. Some of those accidents were fatal.

I could write an entire chapter on the perils these people face just to get where they are going and the perils they face once they make it there. From the extremely dangerous trek over rocky high desert mountains to the constant fear of getting caught, the lives of these people are at risk on a daily basis. They also place the lives of many Americans at risk. The situation that causes these dangers simply must stop. Granting amnesty, in any form, is not the answer; it will only make matters worse. Even though it requires making tough decisions to properly bring it about, I firmly believe there is a workable solution.

Many supporters of Obama's plan for immigration reform claim, as he does, that the United States is a nation of immigrants—a melting pot—represented by many people of the world. I understand and agree with that claim. But I also understand there comes a time in the course of a nation's development where it inevitably takes on its own identity. This nation has long since reached that point. To clarify, I will look at nations as if they were companies.

Most people in this country work for someone else and therefore are required to work under that company's rules and regulations. But let's say you—or perhaps a group of you—wish to form your own company and work under your own rules. To be successful, you must first find a product or service that is marketable and then find a cost-effective and efficient way of producing it. Then you must obtain the financial support to get your business off the ground. Once that is achieved, you must file the necessary paperwork with the appropriate people to declare your desire for business and financial independence.

Although the early going is tough and requires more work than you may sometimes think its worth, you forge on, and eventually, your business begins to grow. As it grows, you reach a point where you need to expand, not only with equipment but also with people. You place an ad stating all who wish to help your company grow and are willing to do the necessary work are welcome to apply. Scores of people from all walks of life show up on your doorstep. You hire as many as you can, but eventually, you run out of positions. Although your employee base is comprised of a highly diverse group of people, your company has become one *family* all working toward a common goal.

Your company continues to grow, and after years of success, you find your once small shop has grown into the strongest and most successful corporation in the world. You now have nearly three hundred million good hardworking employees and a staff of executives to help you manage your company and, as it was from the beginning, with you as its owner.

But then something happens. Over a period of time, you begin to realize that your executives have allowed a dangerous hiring practice to emerge. Instead of maintaining an effective employee base of around three hundred million, your executives have allowed an additional twelve to twenty million to be added to the payroll. To compensate, they have hired the new employees at a lower wage and forced some of the regular employees to cut back on their hours or take time off to reduce the payroll to normal levels.

Although the new employees are hardworkers as well, they are forced to work harder over fears of being replaced by the regular employees waiting at home to be called back to work or by new workers looking to be hired. Forcing employees to work at such a pace can, and often does, lead to accidents in the workplace as well as a decrease in overall productivity. It also takes up too much of the company's infrastructure because the increasing number of new employees is growing faster than the company.

As the owner faced with this knowledge, what do you need to do? You have two choices. You can expand on this concept and eventually replace all your regular employees with the new ones who may or may not have the proper skills to do the job forcing them to work under unsafe conditions, or you can make the smart choice.

Although you hate the thought of doing so, you lay off the new employees, restore the regular employees—who were there from the start, helping your business become successful—to their previous full time positions and order your executives to immediately stop the irresponsible hiring practices and unsafe working conditions.

If you don't, your once-mighty company will eventually fail and all your employees will be unemployed, which helps no one. You also advise the new employees that as your company grows even stronger, you will be more than happy to hire them back on an as-needed basis. At that future time, they will come back to work with full pay under safe and productive working conditions.

This decision may not be popular with the new employees, or even with some of the regular employees who have compassion for those who are now unemployed. As the owner, however, it is the decision you must make if you wish to save not only your company but also the jobs of your employees as well, both current and future. As for the executives who put you and your company in this situation, fire them and replace them with others who will act more responsibly.

Again, President Obama is not the first to call for immigration reform. The previous administration attempted to pass similar legislation. Both former presidents Bush and President Obama at least publicly appear to be compassionate about the plight of illegal aliens. President Obama says he wishes to create a path to citizenship for millions of immigrants so they can finally come out of the shadows. I am not questioning his compassion for these people. What I *am* concerned about are his political motives and the motives of his party.

After considering the testimony given by Dr. Camarota, it doesn't take much to see how a political party could easily take advantage of millions of people who currently can't vote, but by their mere presence will reshape congressional district lines. By changing congressional district lines to their advantage, it becomes easier to get members of their party elected to Congress. Making the path to citizenship a simple one ensures a loyal vote for generations for whichever party creates that path—at least in theory. It also encourages millions more to enter the country illegally in hopes of eventually getting the same deal. We would not be able to build a fence high enough or put enough electronic surveillance devices and personnel in place to stop the mass of people who would flood across our borders every day. It is nearly impossible to do that today. In fact, Border Patrol agents only catch a very small percentage of those who currently cross our borders illegally.

Reshaping congressional district lines to favor one particular party could ensure a total control of power for that party for decades. For those of you who are Democrats—considering the majority your party currently has in Washington—having that advantage may sound like a great idea. Before you jump on board with that notion, what if it were the Republicans who had this advantage?

In 2007, homeland security efforts to enforce immigration laws were at a modest level. President Bush was strongly backing a Republican plan in Congress to pass legislation that would tighten security of our borders through an increase of electronic surveillance and personnel, enforcement of laws against employers who hire illegal aliens, and by granting citizenship to those already in this country. The legislation was eventually defeated by a primarily Democratic-controlled Congress.

Apparently seeing the writing on the wall that Republicans were about to lose control in Washington, coupled with the knowledge of the fast approaching 2010 census, almost immediately after the bill was defeated DHS secretary Michael Chertoff beefed up enforcement of immigration laws to the point that by 2008 some analysts believed the illegal alien population had been significantly reduced.

In the national elections later that year, the Democrats gained a large number of seats in Congress and won the presidential race giving their party full control. Within the first few months of Obama's presidency, Speaker of the House Nancy Pelosi condemned the efforts of ICE agents to enforce immigration laws as being "un-American" and publically called for an end to ICE raids before a mostly Hispanic audience.

DHS secretary Janet Napolitano delayed a series of ICE raids and other workplace actions aimed at finding illegal workers. President Obama continued vowing to fulfill his campaign promise for "comprehensive immigration reform" similar to that supported by President Bush.

Later in 2009, Obama announced immigration reform would be put off until 2010 because of priorities given to the debate over health-care reform. And don't forget about events taking place in 2010: the census and the midterm elections for several seats in Congress. If the Democrats fail to get their version of immigration reform by way of amnesty passed, and they begin to see the writing on the wall of a return to Republican dominance, don't be surprised to see enforcement efforts on employers suddenly increase as well.

If the Republican and Democratic leaders of our nation are so concerned about people who only wish to make a better life for themselves and their families, why do they continue to use them as political pawns? And why are they willing to put American workers in unemployment lines while doing so? Playing politically correct games with people's lives on both sides of the border in order to ensure long-term control for your political party is what I call un-American.

Although I do not support an open-door policy in regard to immigration reform, I do believe the current policies we have are too strict. In order for an immigrant to enter this country legally and eventually become a citizen, they must often wait several years, fill out mountains of paperwork, and spend thousands of dollars. Even then, there are no guarantees they will actually become citizens. I think this practice is unfair. While I agree anyone who wishes to become a citizen must first prove their commitment, I do not agree that commitment should carry such a heavy burden. It is this burden that usually convinces people to enter this country illegally in the first place.

We could also change our current system favorably for those who don't wish to become citizens—who are instead only seeking employment. For example, we could issue a limited number of work visas only when unemployment rates are below a certain level in a particular geographical area, or in special circumstances such as agricultural areas that depend heavily on migrant workers. That way, American workers are not left out in the cold while certain business owners fill the positions that Americans truly don't want. To prevent abuse of the system, ICE agents must be allowed to do their jobs by aggressively enforcing the laws already in place against companies who hire people here illegally.

As I see it, the main difference between the fictitious company I described and this country is that the United States is *employee* owned. This means the people of this great nation are the bosses, and it is the executives (politicians) who work for us. If politicians make bad decisions, regardless of their intent, then we as the owners of this nation need to fire them and hire someone who will act more responsibly. We should also make sure their replacements have the best interests of the country and its people in mind, rather than their own political agendas.

When considering immigration reform, it is vitally important that as a nation that we adopt the same business approach I described. We must adopt a plan where American workers—the backbone on which this country was built—are given top priority for American jobs. In doing so, just as with the company, this country will continue to grow stronger. In turn, this creates more jobs for those from other countries who are seeking a better life. Once here legally, they have a much greater chance of finding it. Everybody wins.

I believe President Obama's current immigration reform policy, as well as the one previously supported by former president Bush, would not only hurt the citizens of this nation but also those they claim to be so concerned about as well.

As Americans, we take pride in the fact that this country was built by a melting pot of immigrants. We celebrate our heritages and honor the cultures of our ancestors with holidays, parades and festivals. These events are open not only to people of a particular heritage but also to all who wish to share in the celebration. We remember with pride the achievements of our ancestors who worked hard to build this great nation. We invite new immigrants to join us in the challenges we face in building the future. But there is one thing we should also remember: if a melting pot continues to be filled without proper supervision and control, it becomes too full, spills over, catches fire, and burns down the house. Then we are all out in the cold.

Fourth recommendation: Eliminate political parties

George Washington warned the American public about forming political parties in his farewell address of 1796 when he said,[64]

> *All obstructions to the execution of the Laws, all combinations and associations, under whatever plausible character, with the real design to direct, control, counteract, or awe the regular deliberation and action*

of the constituted authorities, are destructive of this fundamental principle, and of fatal tendency. They serve to organize faction, to give it an artificial and extraordinary force; to put, in the place of the delegated will of the nation, the will of a party, often a small but artful and enterprising minority of the community; and, according to the alternate triumphs of different parties, to make the public administration the mirror of the ill-concerted and incongruous projects of faction, rather than the organ of consistent and wholesome plans digested by common counsels, and modified by mutual interests.

We should have listened.

Some historians claim George Washington was a member of the Federalist Party. Others believe this to be untrue and claim that the Federalist Party was formed by Alexander Hamilton during Washington's first term. They claim Hamilton built a network of supporters, largely urban, to support his policies of a fiscally sound and strong nationalistic government. This network eventually became the Federalist Party. Those historians also suggest that although Washington was largely sympathetic to the Federalist Party, he remained an independent his entire presidency. After reading Washington's farewell address, I agree.

We commonly refer to the party system in the United States as being a *two-party* system. In reality, there are several political parties in this country with several ideologies. The reason we call it a two-party system is because there are only two parties with enough members and financial backing to realistically have the ability to consistently elect their respective members to major public offices.

During presidential election campaigns, these two parties—Democratic Party (left-wing or liberal) and Republican Party (right-wing or conservative)—hold a series of elections called primaries (or caucuses) to determine their respective nominees who then run against each other in the general election.

One of the problems with this system is those who are not members of either party are left with limited choices on election day.

Candidates for offices other than the president are usually determined by local party committees. Too often, the choices they leave us with under both methods are poor choices indeed.

Supporters of the two-party system claim by having two often widely opposing views forces debate and eventually leads to a compromise, which ends up being in the best interest of all. I believe the truth is, elected officials are frequently more concerned with supporting the agendas of their political and financial backers than they are about truly representing the people who elected them. On the rare occasions, when they do reach a so-called *bipartisan* compromise, the terms of that compromise actually have more to do with helping the *friends* of both parties than helping the people.

When I say we should eliminate political parties, I am not suggesting creating a law that makes them illegal. First of all, attempting to do so would involve the very people who benefit most from political parties, which means it would never happen. Secondly, if by some miracle it did happen, any such law would be unconstitutional on many levels. The good news is, to eliminate political parties, we do not need a law at all. All we need to do is vote wisely.

For generations, many people in this country have voted according to party lines. They vote for the candidate of their favorite party solely because he or she is that party's candidate. They do so for various reasons such as they believe their party always has the best candidates or because of something as simple as family tradition, even if a particular politician's views don't actually match their party's platform. It has been said, "A man who acts as his own attorney has a fool for a client." A political party that has this kind of unconditional support from its base has fools for members.

There has been a slow but growing movement by many in this country to abandon the restricting ideologies of the left and the right. These people are called independents because they vote for the candidate they believe will do the best job, or in most cases, the lesser of evils. When the party in power gets voted out in favor of the opposing party, the victorious party will often hail their victory as a *clear mandate of the people* in support of their agenda. The message they didn't get, or more likely don't want to publically admit, is that the people got tired of getting screwed by the first party so voted for the second party in protest because they felt they did not realistically have anyone else to vote for.

When the independent voter considers voting for a candidate outside of the two parties based on shared principles, they are told since that person has virtually no chance of winning, a vote for that candidate would be a wasted one. First of all, there are only two ways a person can waste a vote: (1) when they don't cast it at all and (2) when they don't vote based on principles. Secondly, the people telling them their vote would be wasted are usually members of one of the two main parties who only want to convince the independent to vote for their candidate.

Independent voters who are swayed by this argument usually agree to change their vote because they believe the issues of that particular election are too important to cast a "protest" vote, and therefore must wait until the next election to do so. To those people I offer this thought: the issues of every election are important enough to express your views through your vote. By not voting according to your principles, the message you are really sending is, "Who do I want to screw me next?" How many more elections are you going let go by before your true voice is heard?

The easiest way to send both Democratic and Republican politicians an undeniable message that the people of this country are totally fed up with the political games they play is to vote for someone else. That said, I am not suggesting that you shouldn't vote for a Democrat or Republican if you truly believe them to be the best candidate running. What I am saying is that people should vote who they believe to be the best candidate whether that person belongs to a political party or not.

The primary job of a politician is to get elected. The secondary job of a politician is to get reelected. Again I would remind you that politicians are like flags: they fly in the direction of the prevailing wind. Since the politicians who see that the changing wind will be unable to convince their own parties to change their platforms from left or right to one that is based more on common sense and better reflects the will of the people, they will soon abandon their parties in order to get elected, or reelected.

I don't support forming a third party of independent voters called the Independent Party or anything else. In fact there are already a few political parties in the United States that have the word *independent* in their party's name. Although their initial motives may be pure, I fear eventually they too could give in to the level of corruption that power brings. What we need at all levels of government are politicians who are accountable not to political parties, but to the people.

While the candidate from the two main parties you thought to be the lesser of two evils may not win because of votes being split between too many candidates, don't let that bother you. If a candidate is bad enough to lose because of a split vote, it is probably because that candidate is just plain bad to begin with.

Do you really want to vote for a not-quite-as-bad candidate? And what incentives do the two main parties have to provide us with good candidates if we keep voting for the bad ones?

I don't know about you, but I am tired of being told I only have a choice between two bad candidates. The candidate who gets my vote has to earn it first. I suggest you consider adopting the same attitude; but that decision, just like the one of who to vote for, is yours and yours alone.

By voting independently—voting for the person you believe best shares your principles—you will be sending candidates of all political parties the clear and undeniable message that we the people have had enough of their game-playing at our expense. Eventually, those flags known as politicians and their political parties will come to realize they must change the way they conduct business and either adapt to the changing winds or be blown off the flagpole. Either way, we will have politicians who better represent the true will of the people.

Opponents of my suggestion to vote independently may say that if enough people vote for presidential candidates outside of the two main parties, no one candidate will win enough electoral college votes to win, and the election would then fall to the decision of Congress. They would be correct. But that only provides me with yet another valid argument for the elimination of the electoral college system.

Without the agendas of political parties which are so far apart we must refer to them as left wing or right wing, perhaps the politicians and the people can come together somewhere in the middle. There we would stand a much greater chance of finding real solutions to the problems we face today and the problems we will face in the future.

Some may claim I am delusional and seeking a form of utopia. They are wrong. Utopia is a fictitious world of peace and harmony without problems; it does not exist and never will. I am not suggesting creating a new world at all. I am only suggesting a method by which we can correct *some* of the problems that exist in this one. To those of you who are Democrats or Republicans who wish to—as former president Bush often put it—"stay the course," I ask, "How has that been working out for you?"

I can't help but remember the words of the so-called Serenity Prayer, which reads,

> *God grant me the serenity to accept the things I cannot change; the courage to change the things I can; and the wisdom to know the difference.*

Because of human nature and differing opinions, we will never live in a world without problems. But we can find a workable compromise to some of them. If we start by correcting the main problems, the additional problems, which were created by those main problems, will automatically take care of themselves. When reasonable men and women work together to find workable solutions, good things can happen.

Fifth recommendation: End the mind game of political correctness; think for yourself

If the freedom of speech is taken away then dumb and silent we may be led, like sheep to the slaughter. (George Washington)

We still have freedom of speech in this country, although it is slowly being taken away from us. Some may look at politically based blogs on the Internet and say otherwise. They will say because of the Internet and those blogs, Americans have a greater chance to speak their minds than ever before. That is true. But look closer at what is being said on those blogs. We have become a nation divided over political issues. On the one hand, liberals who claim to have so much compassion for the underdogs accuse conservatives of being unintelligent and paranoid. Instead of considering what others have to say, they are quick to call anyone with opposing views racists or hate-mongers.

On the other hand, conservatives are so busy defending their comments with frustration and anger they forget to properly present their points. If you stop and think about it, neither method shows much in the way of intelligence, and we are all suffering because of it. It appears we already have the dumb part down. The more we give into PC, the closer we get to the silent part. The next logical step would therefore be the slaughterhouse.

So why do we have such a harsh division and who is to blame? Our politicians are, for starters. They constantly create regulations and laws, which in reality, usually only benefit themselves, then attach some politically correct worthy cause terms to the titles to give them false legitimacy for the public. To divide us, they rely on the emotional responses of those who either agree or disagree with a particular cause. We become so busy fighting among ourselves we don't notice that the bills being voted on are actually nothing more than money being given to special interest groups for political payback or worse. This is a classic example of *divide and conquer*, with the public being the ones conquered. Ultimately, it is the people who are at fault because we allow them to get away with it.

As I said in the first chapter, of all the problems we have in this country, the effect of political correctness is the easiest to correct. Unlike my first four suggestions, which require either constitutional amendments or a simultaneous effort of millions, this solution could be done by one person at a time. There is no need to coordinate with scores of people to get them on the same page. If you take the first step toward that solution, others will follow.

Don't let it bother you if those who follow don't share your views on how problems should be solved. Part of the best method of solving problems is to have a wide range of ideas then work together to find the best solution. But it must be done in the spirit of cooperation instead of the divisiveness, which inevitably occurs because of a strict and uncompromising adherence to one's political ideology.

If someone tells you that mothers are being torn from nursing babies, google it. Look for news reports that back up *and* discredit such claims. Then decide for yourself if it is true. If it is true, find out the truth about why it is happening—not just through politically biased news agencies, blogs, forums, or other such media that support your preconceived notions, but through every avenue you can find. Once you have looked at all the evidence with an honest and objective mind, decide for yourself who is telling the truth and who is either misleading you or outright lying to you.

Do the same with every claim that tugs at your heart, makes you angry, or makes you wonder what this world is coming to. I can almost guarantee, you will be surprised at what you find. You may find out, as I have, that some of your preconceived notions are actually not based in fact or are just plain wrong.

Have the courage to recognize the truth, accept it as truth, and then not allow anyone to sway you from it. If someone attempts to do so, ask them specifically where they obtained their information. If they provide you with a source you haven't seen, check it out. It could be something worth considering, or it may not. If they can't provide you with a new source, or simply say they read or heard it somewhere, you are probably talking to a sheep.

For a case in point, we only need to look as far as the new Arizona immigration law (SB1070h).[65]

I first heard about the new law through a pro-immigration media. My initial reaction was, "Oh brother, what have they (Arizona politicians) done now?" I went on to read that according to this article, the new law was an attack on the fourth amendment in regard to the *"no Warrants shall issue, but upon probable cause"* clause.

After reading this article, I decided to go to the official Arizona state website and read the law as it was passed as well as the law (HB2162c),[66] which was passed a week later to amend some of the wording of the original law. After reading these laws, I believe the claims made by the article to be incorrect and very misleading.

SB1070h basically states that no state or local law enforcement agency may approach a person for the express purpose of determining their legal status without first making "*lawful contact.*"

After SB1070h was signed into law, there was some debate over the definition of that term. Sponsors as well as supporters of the law claimed that the term meant a person had to first be suspected or accused of committing a different offense (much like the old seat belt laws), and even then they could only be questioned about their legal status "*where reasonable suspicion exists that the person is an alien who is unlawfully present in the United States.*" I am not a lawyer but the term "*reasonable suspicion,*" as used here, appears to sufficiently satisfy the probable cause requirements of the Fourth Amendment.

Opponents of the law claimed lawful contact *could* be interpreted as a person simply asking an officer for directions among other things. I found this argument to be both fair and valid.

To address this apparent loophole, the Arizona state legislature passed HB2162c, which contains amendments to SB1070h changing some of the wording in the original law.

For example, the phrase "*lawful contact*" was changed to "*lawful stop, detention or arrest*" to clarify that an officer would not be required to question a crime victim or witness about their legal status.

As you can see, this clarification not only reduces the possibility of unintentional mistakes by police officers but also creates a legally better-defined set of hurdles that must be cleared before a person is subjected to questioning in the first place.

The article I read also claims that these laws will open the door for racial profiling. Again I turn to the amendments in HB2162c in conjunction with a little common sense.

SB1070h dealt with the issue of racial profiling by stating,

*A law enforcement official or agency of this state or a
county, city, town or other political subdivision of this
state may not solely consider race, color or national origin
in implementing the requirements of this subsection except
to the extent permitted by the United States or Arizona
Constitution.*

During the debate, opponents of the bill argued that the word
"*solely*" allowed officers to base their reasonable suspicion on race
and color as long as it wasn't just one of them—another fair and
valid point. HB2162c corrects this potential loophole by striking
the word "*solely*"from the sentence. Bill sponsor Sen. Russell Pearce,
representative of Mesa, said the intent of making these changes (in
HB2162c) was to clarify that "*this bill prohibits racial profiling in any
form.*"

Now let us look at this from a real-world perspective. Racial
profiling was illegal before either of these laws were written. Does
racial profiling still exist? Of course, it does. Did SB1070h create
potential loopholes that could have inadvertently allowed racial
profiling? I believe it did. I also believe those potential loopholes
were sufficiently closed by the amendments in HB2162c.

Racial profiling existed before these, or any other laws were
written prohibiting the practice, and yes, it will continue. Not just
in Arizona but the entire country. It will continue because there are
some people in law enforcement who intentionally break the law in
the course of carrying out their duties. I call them bad cops. Perhaps
we as citizens should be focusing more attention on weeding out the
bad cops who break the law rather than falsely accusing the law they
break of giving racial profiling the stamp of legal authority when it
explicitly prohibits it.

In fact, I believe the Arizona law is one of the toughest laws on
the books against racial profiling. I also believe we should also have
a bit more faith in the judgment of the good cops who abide by the
laws of the land.

Humans are naturally reactionary when faced with such topics.
We have a tendency to jump too quickly to conclusions based on our

personal beliefs and/or political ideologies more than actual facts. Or put in simpler terms, we think with our hearts instead our minds. Perhaps we would do better to use both. We should also learn to put aside our preconceived political partisanships—political correctness and the tendency to automatically hate *anything* that comes from the other side—allowing our hearts and minds to do a better job.

Will these laws pass the constitutional test in our courts of law? If the justices involved base their rulings on the letter of the law and not on individual or collective political ideology, I believe it will. But that is just my opinion. Only time will tell.

Many of the opponents of the Arizona law I spoke to haven't actually read it. My question to them was how can you criticize and condemn a law you haven't read? In most cases, their response was because officials in the Obama administration were against it. Since those officials claimed that the law was unconstitutional and promoted racial profiling, similar claims they were hearing in the news must be true.

Although it is always best to consult an attorney when dealing with the legal interpretations of laws, anyone who takes the time to read this law will see that the accusations made against it are unfounded and nothing more than PC rhetoric.

A great many of the people I spoke with also told me privately that they were afraid to speak out in favor of the bill even if the accusations turned out to be false because they didn't want to be seen as being racist. I explained to them that seeking the truth doesn't make someone a racist, but not seeking the truth sometimes can. If I had not sought out the truth in my youth, I would probably still be a racist today.

If someone attempts to make you feel intellectually inferior or calls you names because of what you believe, don't be intimidated. People who use this tactic without providing credible evidence to back up their claims are usually trying to hide one of two things: the truth or their own ignorance. At the end of the day, it is you who must live with your beliefs. Shouldn't those beliefs be based on facts instead of politically correct propaganda?

CHAPTER NINE

The One-Hundred-
Thousand-Dollar Plan

A new revolution is possible only in consequences of a new crisis.

—Karl Marx

From each according to his abilities, to each according to his needs.

—Karl Marx [speaking about the theory of redistribution of wealth]

I think when you spread the wealth around its good for everybody.

—Barrack Obama

Obama made the now-famous comment to "Joe the plumber" while explaining his views of the theory of redistribution of wealth. The first time I saw the clip on television it did not show the entire conversation. I found the full version on the YouTube website and watched it for myself. Some may claim Obama's remarks were taken out of context or exaggerated by the media. If the clip in question had been the only time he had expressed that view, perhaps I would have agreed. But I have also found other comments he has made, which strongly suggest he shares the views of Karl Marx on this subject—at least in principle.

Apparently some of Obama's supporters do as well. These supporters come from many walks of life ranging from members of his administration who advise him or who actually make policy, members of Congress who create laws, filmmakers who preach of the evils of capitalism, artists who use their talent to promote his agenda, those in the entertainment industry who make pledges to be a servant to the President,[67] to average citizens who spread the word throughout their communities.

These people have the right to express themselves in this manner if they so choose. I would advise caution in this practice however.

When you become a servant to politicians, even if you believe doing so is for the good of all mankind, you allow yourself to become a puppet or pawn in the political games played by those who may (and often do) wish to control your every move. And most importantly, you are opening yourself up to the distinct possibility of being brainwashed by them and their agendas. In the end, and often too late, you may find those agendas actually have very little to do with your own. Remember the people in the FLDS have done the same thing. Your devotion may not be as severe as theirs but it is just as dangerous.

If I were to pledge to become a servant to anyone or anything, it would be to the following in this order: me, my family, and mankind. Putting myself first instead of mankind may seem very selfish to some. But I believe it is the first and most important step toward helping mankind. If I don't take care of myself first, both mentally and physically, how can I support my family? If I cannot support my family, how can I possibly believe I can help mankind? Although some of those entertainers pledged to support worthy causes, in the end, what they were doing is using political correctness to promote the propaganda of a politician.

I don't agree with the theory behind redistribution of wealth. I do believe capitalism, even with all its faults, is the best system by which all mankind can prosper. I may not have a degree in economics, but I do know a thing or two about incentive. Although it has been said that necessity is the mother of invention, capitalism is by far the greatest motivator by which the best inventions come about.

The only way for a true redistribution of wealth to occur is for the government to take control of all business—or in a word, communism. Under communism, the people become nothing more than slaves to the government. Unless they have a gun to their heads, people under communist rule lose all incentive to work hard or invent new and improved goods and services. They make barely enough to support themselves and their families and can't even begin to help mankind. Most importantly, they lose their freedoms.

Capitalism is all about profit. Supporters of socialism, Marxism, and communism claim those systems to be all about the people. There have been so-called great philosophers who have either written about, or put into practice these theories. Those philosophers are people such as Karl Marx, Mao Zedong, and Vladimir Lenin. In reality, the practice of their philosophies have been all about a few people—the ruling class.

Redistribution of wealth relies on the premise of Robin Hood—steal from the rich and give to the poor. Under the modern-day version, however, the stealing is done by the taxman instead of a merry band of men in tights.

Under today's plan in the United States, the rich (those who make more than $250,000 a year) would pay the majority of taxes while the poor would receive tax breaks. Sounds great doesn't it? But here is the reality of it: those who are rich are rich for a reason. They know how to make money and how to keep it. In spite of already having some of the highest tax rates of anyone, they also have tax shelters, which legally exempt them from paying most of them. Even if the government removed all the tax shelters from the rich, they would still find a way to get around paying taxes. It is one of the things they do best.

But don't wait for all tax shelters to be removed from the rich any time soon, because the ruling class (politicians) are usually also rich, and they are not about to hurt themselves. In addition, they constantly ask the American people to buckle down during hard economic times but always seem to find the money to give themselves huge pay raises.

So if the rich aren't paying taxes and neither are the rich politicians, who is left to pay them? The answer to that question is the poor and working class, as usual. If you think about it, didn't Robin Hood steal from the rich because the taxman was collecting too many taxes from the poor?

While the modern-day story of Robin Hood (redistribution of wealth) might make for good philosophical debate and literature, as an economic practice, it is a recipe for disaster, which has failed more than once. It has not only failed as a political system but it also has created a much lower standard of living for those under its control.

Opponents of capitalism claim capitalists make their fortunes on the backs of the workers. In theory, I agree. But the same could be said of any economic system. If you have doubts, ask people from the former Soviet Union how they enjoyed working for a communist government.

A good capitalist knows the value of a good worker and if they are smart, they will reward their workers with decent wages and benefits in order to keep them. If you have good workers, you stand a far greater chance of making more profit. If you are a good worker who works for a good capitalist, you already *share the wealth* and provide for your family through decent wages, benefits, and working conditions.

Another benefit of capitalism is the expansion of the national economy through an increase of jobs. As an example, I will use the very tool I am using to write this book, a home computer. Computers have been around for many years now. But it was not until Apple developed a computer system that was designed for home use that most of us ever had the chance to use one.

Because it was a new type of system, the cost of a home computer was expensive to say the least. Over time, the price fell somewhat, but not enough for most Americans to afford one. Then along came a man named Bill Gates.

Gates's company, Microsoft, developed a new operating system for home computers called Windows. This new development gave home computer buyers a choice instead of being compelled to purchase from only one company. Over time, the new-found competition from a second company forced home computer prices to drop, putting them within the reach of the average consumer and creating new innovations in the industry. Over the years, both Apple and Microsoft grew into major companies employing thousands of people.

However, the story didn't stop there. Hundreds of support companies—software, computer accessory, and hardware companies, etc.—either came into existence or expanded because of the affordability of home computers. Some of those companies grew to be rather large as well: Hewlett Packard, Intel, America Online, and Cisco Systems, just to name a few. Each of these companies employs hundreds if not thousands of people, usually with well-paying jobs.

Because of his capitalist nature, Bill Gates has become one of the richest men in the world. Supporters of the redistribution of wealth theory have claimed Gates has too much money, that no man has the right to have that much money and he should spread the wealth to those in need. To support this claim, they ask, "How much does one person need to live anyway?"

Not to take away anything from Steve Jobs and Steven Wozniak (cofounders of Apple) who brought us the home computer in the first place, but a man who creates competition in an industry, which eventually creates so many new companies and all those new jobs deserves to be financially rewarded. If you think about it, the competition between Apple and Microsoft has probably generated more revenue and good paying jobs than our government has, and they are only two companies in one industry.

To those who support the redistribution of wealth, I have a few questions. If the government had controlled the entire computer industry prior to the home computer, do you think they would have created the competition and jobs that Apple and Microsoft did? Do you think we would have a home computer industry or a public Internet at all? If not, what makes you think the government, in the interest of redistributing wealth, would be the best to run *any* industry? That is why many of us who oppose your view advise you to get off your butts and go out and invent your own operating system if you want a piece of Bill Gates's wealth.

Some may argue that communist China currently has a stronger economy than the United States and we should therefore adopt their plan. It may be true China's economy is currently stronger, but who in China benefits the most from their strong economy, the common citizen or the ruling class? If you take a closer look at how the Chinese government has built that wealth, you'll find they have done it through open market trade with other countries like the United States. This is nothing more than international capitalism via a communist-controlled workforce. The ruling class and the fat-cat businessmen get richer while the working class suffers. So who is making their fortunes off the backs of the workers there?

Given the choice, I would rather work in a capitalist society where I have the freedom to change jobs if I feel I am not being treated the way I should, rather than in a communist one where I don't have that freedom. The key word in that last sentence being *freedom*. It simply makes good economic and social sense.

Some supporters of wealth redistribution are millionaires who have benefited from the very capitalist system they condemn. Capitalism has its flaws and is by no means perfect—there is still corruption and mismanagement, but until someone comes along with a better system, I'll stick with the only one that actually works for most who choose to engage in it.

However, in the interest of fairness, I have developed a plan, which will possibly help wealthy redistributionists change people's minds. I call it "The One-Hundred-Thousand-Dollar Plan." To help you show all Americans that the theory of redistribution of wealth is the way to go, I challenge each and every redistributionist to adopt this plan. Here is how it works:

Each redistributionist who, in total assets, is worth $250,000 or more will become income tax exempt for the next twenty years. But they must agree to liquidate all their assets and turn them into cash with the exception of one of their homes. They will keep the one remaining home to live in, unless that home is too large for them to support under this plan. If so, they must sell that house also and buy one which they can afford.

Liquidating all assets means selling everything: homes, boats, planes, investment properties, stocks, bonds, etc. They must sell everything that has value now, or may have value in the future without having someone hold on to it till after the twenty-year period is over. This will be monitored by a team of accountants and lawyers.

Once this is accomplished, each redistributionist must place all their money into one bank account. They must then write a check in the amount of $100,000 (or the balance of what is left) to each of the poorest families in the United States until they themselves are left with no more than $100,000 to live off of for a year. Now when I say *live off of for a year*, it means they must pay for everything with only the $100,000 each of them has left, and only one bank account per family. They cannot accept a single gift from anyone of any kind, nor can they benefit in any way from an expense account of any kind. One account of $100,000 total to live on for the entire year, period. Think about it: how much does a person really need to live anyway? The poor families they give the money to can do with that money as they see fit except give any of it back.

Each of those redistributionists must continue to work hard, if not even harder, to make as much money as possible during that year. All the money earned will be placed in another bank account to be distributed in the same manner the following year—i.e., $100,000 goes to the redistributionist's family and the rest goes to another group of poorest families, and so forth—for twenty years.

As you might imagine, with the collective billions of dollars from wealthy redistributionist's money being redistributed at the rate of $100,000 per year, the number of poor families in this country would be next to nothing if not eliminated within twenty years.

Of course, there is the problem of each of those poor families eventually running out of money and going back to being poor, unless they use it to invest in themselves and get good-paying jobs to ensure financial security for their families. Unfortunately, there will also be certain poor families who choose to squander their newfound wealth by buying a new big-screen TV, new furniture, a new computer, or a $24,000 electric car. By the way, they will be unable to afford to electrically charge those cars because under President Obama's Cap and Trade Bill, utility prices—as Obama himself said—will "necessarily skyrocket."[68]

So what do you say? Are you in? Are you willing to put your own money where your mouth is?

In spite of all these realities, if you, Mr. President, those in your administration, members of Congress, people in the entertainment industry, and other servants to the president will *all* accept the challenge of my plan, I will pledge to take another hard and honest look at yours. If you are not, then shut the hell up and go back to your day jobs.

To those of you in the White House and Congress, start doing your day job the right way—not the way you have been doing it. For example, don't create legislation that will force people to purchase the health insurance *you* determine they should have and then fine them if they don't.

Opinion polls have shown most Americans did want health-care reform. In my opinion, the current law has more to do with massive tax hikes than providing health care for those who can't afford it. Americans don't want massive tax hikes. Another thing Americans don't want is politicians preying on our compassion for the underdog by calling these tax increases *health-care reform* in order to gain public support and make themselves look good in the process.

What we really need is viable health-care reform in this country that actually works and we aren't getting it under the current law.

Currently my wife and I are two of the millions of Americans who make too much money to get free health care (free clinics and hospitals) but not enough to afford health insurance—you know, two of the people this law is supposed to help. Since the passage of this law, we will have no choice but to pay the fines because even if insurance rates do drop somewhat they will still be out of our reach. So who are they really helping? And why do politicians need to spend nearly one trillion dollars for a bill that won't really help anyone but themselves?

Of course, I don't actually believe anyone will take me up on my plan. Why would they? They make is sound as if the wealth that will be redistributed will come from those who have the most of it. As I said before, the rich are very adept at holding on to their money. Even if the government could manage to find a way to become modern-day Robin Hoods and steal from the rich to give to the poor, the rich would only pass those costs on to the consumer. The middle class would ultimately pay the price while the rich would continue being rich.

Eventually, the burden would become financially overwhelming for the middle class and would drive their standard of living down to the equivalent of the poor. Just as in communist countries, this would leave us with only two classes of people: the ruling class and the poor.

Don't be fooled into thinking redistribution of wealth is intended to be limited to this country. If you listen closely to what

Ron Walker

many supporters also say, it doesn't take long to figure out that their ultimate goal is to redistribute American wealth globally to third-world nations. Realistically, there is no way to increase the wages of workers in third-world countries to American standards. The poorest people in this country would be considered rich by third-world standards. The only way that wages can be brought to a more uniform global standard is to increase the standards of poorer countries to a limited degree while dramatically reducing the American standards.

Take some time to research the so-called *New World Order*, theories of global governance and the global redistribution of wealth through carbon exchange fees via laws such as cap and trade. Then consider how using the alleged crisis of man-caused global warming could easily be used to persuade people to go along with such ideas. After all, who would not want to save the planet from burning up?

Money equals power and there is only a certain amount of power to be had in this world. When someone loses power, it doesn't evaporate into the sky, it shifts to someone else. The more powerful people become, the more corrupt they become. If we allow a redistribution of wealth in this country to occur and the already powerful become even more powerful, what do you think would happen to the average American then? Now consider what would happen if global redistribution were to occur.

If you think that redistributing the wealth is merely a way of punishing the rich in order to help the poor, why then are there so many rich people supporting this plan?

Looking at issues such as cap and trade, the health-care reform law and redistribution of wealth individually are spooky enough. Collectively they become downright frightening. It would be wise for us to remember the words of the former leader of the Soviet Union, Nikita Khrushchev:

> *We can't expect the American people to jump from capitalism to communism, but we can assist their elected leaders in giving them small doses of socialism, until they awaken one day to find that they have communism.*

190

He also said that communism would take over America *without firing a shot*. Khrushchev and the Soviet Union may be gone, but apparently, their ideals remain. But instead of only keeping a watchful eye on foreign nations as we have in the past, perhaps we should also be paying more attention to the people in our own country who have similar ideals. Because in case you haven't been paying attention, their ideals seem to be winning, one small dose at a time.

Chapter Ten

A Word Of Thanks

Ask not what your country can do for you. Ask what you can do for your country.

—John F. Kennedy

Before I conclude, I would like to take a moment to acknowledge a few people who have given me the courage to say what I mean and mean what I say and to question that which doesn't seem right. People are the sum of their own experiences. It is the people we meet, the places we go, the things we do, and the things done to us that help make us who we are today. I am no exception. To all the people whose paths I have crossed in one way or another, thank you for helping me to be the person I am today.

The following are some of those people:

Charles R. Walker Sr., my father:

You taught me by example to always do my best, to be fair, honest, and to live my life with integrity, not only when dealing with others but also with myself as well. Although it took a while for me to fully understand the latter, I finally got there. You are no longer with us in this world, but it gives me comfort to know I will see you in the next. You may be gone, but never forgotten.

Blanche Alice Walker, my mother:

There are many reasons why I love and respect you. But if I had to choose one, it would be your undying strength and courage to tell it like it is. Or how you usually so eloquently put it, "How the cow ate the cabbage." You may not express your views in the most diplomatic fashion, but you are usually right—except when you fuss at me (just kidding). I could say you have mellowed a great deal in your old age, but I would be lying. But hey, at least I inherited the trait of telling it like it is honestly.

Susannah A. Walker, my best friend and wife:

Because there are people like you in the world, I still have hope for the future. Your love of life, your willingness to love, your ability to light up the faces in a room with your mere presence, and your infectious smile do not even begin to explain the many reasons why I love you and want to grow old with you. Thank you for your patience while I attempt to live my dream. Thank you for putting up with my occasional stubbornness. Okay, maybe my stubbornness wasn't quite so *occasional*, but I digress. But most of all, thank you for being you and allowing this old guy to tag along for the ride.

Jessica Walker Catchpole, my daughter:

You may have gotten your passion for animals from your mother, but you got your sense of humor from me (just go with it, people are watching). I am so happy for you that you have finally found happiness, and you have achieved so many of your dreams.

Although I am glad you are getting the opportunity to live in so many places throughout Europe, I do miss seeing you. You have your own life to live now and I wish you and Ian all the continued happiness you can find. But no matter where the two of you find yourselves in the years to come, never forget how proud I am of you both, and that you will always be Papa's little girl.

Elaine Jeffs, my mother-in-law:

There are many people who say they would do something dangerous to protect their family if it became necessary, but few ever do. You are one of the few. I have always admired you for who you are, and what you did for your children. Most men cringe when they hear their mother-in-law is coming for a visit, but I am grateful for having the chance to get to know you. In our house, you are always welcome.

Charles F. Padget, author and friend:

Although we may not always agree, your willingness to call it as you see it in today's politically correct society is one of the things that gave me inspiration to take on the challenges of this endeavor. Most reading this may not understand, but we are even, Brother.

There is one last person I wish to thank, although I won't mention her name. I will never forget the three sentences she told me at a time when I was at the lowest point in my life. "Trust your gut. Think for yourself. You'll know what to do." If she ever reads this, she will know who she is. She will also know I listened.

When it is all said and done, those three sentences are exactly what I am trying to say to you, the reader. Don't give in to peer pressure because you're afraid of what your friends might think of you. Don't blindly accept something you see on television, hear from your friends or on the radio, or read in the newspaper, online, or in books as truth just because *they* say so. I will let you in on a secret: *they* often have no clue as to what *they* are talking about, or *they* are trying to sell you something. Don't buy it. And I won't ask you to take my word for it or even agree with my views. Challenge what you hear, research things for yourself, then make up your own mind.

I tell you all this because I am one of you. I have lived most of my life doing the same as you. I have never, not once, ever written my congressman to let him or her know how I feel. I have always been a person who says, "What is this world coming to?" whenever I heard about another small dose of socialism being given to our leaders, but did nothing about it. In short, I have not been a good patriot. But that ends today.

Stating my views here is my first step toward taking President Kennedy's advice by doing something for my country. But by the grace of God (and, yes, I did say "God"), it won't be the last. It is only a suggestion, but your first step could be as simple as no longer allowing political correctness to control your heart, your mind, do your thinking for you, or allowing it to take away your freedoms. That is entirely up to you. Trust your gut. Think for yourself. You'll know what to do.

I wish to thank you for taking the time to read this book. I hope you find it helpful in your endeavors.

Now if you will excuse me, I have a letter to write to my congressman. And come to think of it, there are a couple of senators who need to hear from me as well.

INDEX

A

Adams, Brooke, 27, 205
"Listening to the Lord: Jeffs
exerted 24-7 control over
FLDS faithful," 27
Adams, John Quincy, 145, 157
African American, 20, 53, 55
Alinsky, Saul, 137
American Civil Liberties Union,
71, 208
American Civil War, 68
American Indians, 98-100
Americans, average, 20
Americans United for Separation
of Church and State, 101
amnesty, 122-23, 165, 168
Anderson, J. Morris, 48-49
Anderson, John William, 72
Andrews, Edna, 59, 207
"Cultural Sensitivity and Political
Correctness: The Linguistic
Problem of Naming," 59
Arizona immigration law, 177-80,
213
Aryan-Nordic people, 59

B

baby killers, 65, 67
Baer, Kenneth, 73
Batiz-Aceves, Santana, 86
Baton Rouge, 13, 16
beauty pageants, 48, 50, 52-53.
See also Miss Black America
Bejarano, Brittney, 128
Bill of Rights, 150. See also
Constitution
Blinder, Martin, 37
blood atonement, 26, 32
Bluewater's Santa Boot Camp, 95
Borden, Marcus, 101

British Airways, 91
Brown, Daniel, 71
Burr, Aaron, 156
Bush, George W., 68-69, 158,
168, 170, 175
Bush, John Ellis "Jeb," 158
Bush's Brain (Moore), 71

C

California State Legislature, 37
Camarota, Steven A., 160-61,
163, 167, 206
Campbell-Reilly, Fiona, 95
capitalism, 182-87
Casey, Kathy, 93
Cash, David, 97
caucuses, 171. See also primaries
Cavanaugh, Dennis, 101
Center for Immigration Studies,
160, 162, 206, 212
Chandler Rapist, 85-86, 90
Chertoff, Michael, 168
Chisholm, Alexander, 58
Chisholm v. Georgia, 58
Class Divided, A (Peters), 55, 207
Cleveland, Grover, 157
Clinton, Hillary, 74
Cold War, 61
communism, 61, 63, 183, 191
comprehensive immigration
reform, 40, 121-23, 168
Condit Elementary School, 96
congressional redistricting, 159-
60, 163, 167
Conservatives. See Republican Party
Countdown, 137
Cultural Revolution, 60
"Cultural Sensitivity and Political
Correctness: The Linguistic
Problem of Naming"
(Andrews), 59, 207

Sources

1. Berry Knoll's FLDS 101 website "FLDS History 101—Self proclaimed Prophet"
    http://flds101.blogspot.com/2008/05/flds-history-101-self-appointed-prophet.html

    Telegraph.co.uk, September 14, 2007 "Prophet on trial for forcing girl to marry cousin" Catherine Elsworth
    http://www.telegraph.co.uk/news/worldnews/1563130/Prophet-on-trial-for-forcing-girl-to-marry-cousin.html

2. Berry Knoll's FLDS 101 website "FLDS Beliefs 101—Force or Choice"
    http://flds101.blogspot.com/2008/05/flds-beliefs-101-force-or-choice.html

3. The Salt Lake Tribune, March 5, 2009 "Listening to the Lord: Jeffs exerted 24-7 control over FLDS faithful," Brooke Adams. Note: A copy of this article can be obtained from the archives of the online version of this newspaper for a small fee.
    http://www.sltrib.com/

4. *http://www.merriam-webster.com/dictionary/political%20correctness*

5. *http://en.wikipedia.org/wiki/Political_correctness*

6. *The San Francisco Chronicle, November 23, 2003 "Myth of the 'Twinkie defense'* The verdict in the Dan White case wasn't based on his ingestion of junk food" Carol Pogash
    http://www.sfgate.com/cgi-bin/article.cgi?f=/c/a/2003/11/23/INGRE343501.DTL

7. Wikipedia Ariticle entitled, "Twinkie defense"
   http://en.wikipedia.org/wiki/Twinkie_defense

   "The reign of error: psychiatry, authority, and law" page 69, Lee Coleman, Deacon Press, 1984
   http://books.google.com/books?ei=UfCwTIGTIIHSsAOXq-3tCw&ct=result&id=O2nuAAAAMAAJ&dq=George+Solomon+dan+white+twinkie+defense&q=sort+of+on+automatic+pilot#search_anchor

8. People's Advocate website California Proposition #8, "Criminal Justice" passed in 1982.
   http://www.peoplesadvocate.org/prop8.html

9. The Federation for American Immigration Reform, "Remittances to Mexico"
   http://www.fairus.org/site/News2?page=NewsArticle&id=20897

10. Center for Immigration Studies, November 2007 "Immigrants in the United States, 2007" Steven A. Camarota
    http://www.cis.org/articles/2007/back1007.html

11. Old Miss Black America website's "History" page.
    http://www.missblackamerica.com/MBAHistory.htm

12. "Out of the mouths of slaves: African American language and education" page 86 John Baugh
    http://books.google.com/books?id=xoZOPOyF2YkC&pg=PA86&lpg=PA86&dq=jesse+jackson+african+american+cultural+base&source=bl&ots=nEFSRzdT4Z&sig=oQ2lSr7NwQtkRTBDzLrv-c9WFIU&hl=en&ei=blsOSqudNOawtgfcu_iGCA&sa=X&oi=book_result&ct=result&resnum=7#v=onepage&q=jesse%20jackson%20african%20american%20cultural%20base&f=false

    In These Times website, Febuary 21, 2007 "A Politically Correct Lexicon" Joel Bleifuss
    http://www.inthesetimes.com/article/3027/a_politically_correct_lexicon/

13. PBS Frontline "One Friday in April, 1968"
    http://www.pbs.org/wgbh/pages/frontline/shows/divided/etc/friday.html

14. PBS Frontline "A Class Divided"
    http://www.pbs.org/wgbh/pages/frontline/shows/divided/etc/faq.html

15. PBS Frontline "A Class Divided"
    http://www.pbs.org/wgbh/pages/frontline/shows/divided/

16. MLK Online "I Have a Dream - Address at March on Washington"
    http://www.mlkonline.net/dream.html

17. Find Law website, "U.S. Supreme Court: Chisholm v. State of GA., 2 U.S. 419 (1793)
    http://caselaw.lp.findlaw.com/scripts/getcase.pl?court=us&vol=2&invol=419

18. "Cultural Sensitivity and Political Correctness: The Linguistic Problem of Naming," Edna Andrews, *American Speech*, Vol. 71, No. 4 (Winter, 1996), pp. 389-404.
    http://www.jstor.org/pss/455713

19. Jewish Virtual Library, "Chronology of Jewish Persecution: 1933"
    http://www.jewishvirtuallibrary.org/jsource/Holocaust/Chronology_1933.html

20. Archive.org Full text on "Mein Kampf" (Although I found slightly different wording attributed to this quote, the basic idea remained the same as quoted here.)
    http://www.archive.org/stream/meinkampf035176mbp/meinkampf035176mbp_djvu.txt

21. President Harry Truman, Robert H. Ferrell, "The Autobiography of Harry S. Truman", Boulder: University Press of Colorado. October 1, 1980

22. Wikipedia article on the Vietnam War which includes casualty figures as of May 11, 2010
    http://en.wikipedia.org/wiki/Vietnam_War_casualties

    Congressional Research Service PDF
    http://www.fas.org/sgp/crs/natsec/RL32492.pdf

23. Encyclopedia Britannica website "George W. Bush: Declaration of War on Terrorism" Speech delivered on September 20, 2001 to a joint session of Congress.
http://www.britannica.com/presidents/article-9398253

24. USA PATRIOT ACT OF 2001.
http://frwebgate.access.gpo.gov/cgi-bin/getdoc.cgi?dbname=107_cong_public_laws&docid=f:publ056.107

25. American Civil Liberties Union website "Unlikely Suspects"
http://www.aclu.org/technology-and-liberty/unlikely-suspects

26. The Washington Post, March 25, 2009 "'Global War on Terror' Is Given New Name" Scott Wilson and Al Kamen
http://www.washingtonpost.com/wp-dyn/content/article/2009/03/24/AR2009032402818.html

The Los Angeles Times, March 26, 2009 "Obama administration snuffs global war on terror (the term anyway)" Andrew Malcolm
http://latimesblogs.latimes.com/washington/2009/03/obama-words.html

Fox News, March 25, 2009 "Obama Scraps 'Global War on Terror' for 'Overseas Contingency Operation'"
http://www.foxnews.com/politics/2009/03/25/obama-scraps-global-war-terror-overseas-contingency-operation/

27. Spiegle Online International website, March 16, 2009 "Away From the Politics of Fear"
http://www.spiegel.de/international/world/0,1518,613330,00.html

28. Department of Homeland Security Report on "Rightwing Extremism" leaked in 2009
http://www.fas.org/irp/eprint/rightwing.pdf

29. The Washington Post, July 2, 1995, Page A01 "An Ordinary Boy's Extraordinary Rage" Dale Russakoff and Serge F. Kovaleski
http://www.washingtonpost.com/wp-srv/national/longterm/oklahoma/bg/mcveigh.htm

30. Text of H.R. 3355 "Violent Crime Control and Law Enforcement Act of 1994" SEC. 280003 (a)
    http://thomas.loc.gov/cgi-bin/query/F?c103:1:./
    temp/~c103aOGRfD:e927518:

31. East Valley Tribune, Posted online, November 10, 2007 12:00 am updated March 10, 2010 11:53 am "Calling rapist a Hispanic irks radio station"
    http://www.eastvalleytribune.com/article_6062f82d-1a1e-56c1-bc98-e3cb50ede8c8.html

    Fox News, November 14, 2007 "Spanish-Language Radio Station Slams Police for Describing Suspect as 'Hispanic'" Melissa Underwood
    http://www.foxnews.com/story/0,2933,311717,00.html

32. PDF copy of correspondence between Los Abogados Hispanic Bar Association and Arizona Supreme Court Chief Justice Ruth V. McGregor September 12, 2008 to October 2, 2008
    http://content.clearchannel.com/cc-common/
    mlib/616/11/616_1226359587.pdf

33. World Net Daily, October 15, 2006 "Airline bans woman from wearing cross" Michael Ireland
    http://www.wnd.com/news/article.asp?ARTICLE_ID=52447

34. Save Our Country Now website, posted March 30, 2009 "Connecticut School Bans Physical Contact"
    http://www.saveourcountrynow.net/archives/1186

35. Fox News, November 8, 2007 "Students Feel the Squeeze as Schools Ban Hugs" Sara Bonisteel
    http://www.foxnews.com/story/0,2933,309296,00.html

36. WHDH News Boston, MA, October 13, 2007 "Witch noose hanging decoration causes controversy"
    http://www3.whdh.com/news/articles/local/BO64410/

37. Fox News, November 15, 2007 "Australian Santas Asked Not to 'Ho Ho Ho'" Janet Fyfe-Yeomans and Amanda Grant
    http://www.foxnews.com/story/0,2933,311797,00.html

38. Mail Online "Santa told to slim down for Christmas to 'set a good example'" Last updated November 5, 2007
   http://www.dailymail.co.uk/news/article-491770/Santa-told-slim-Christmas-set-good-example.html

39. The Los Angeles Times, November 25, 2008 "Insulting stereotype, or harmless holiday feast?" Seema Mehta
   http://articles.latimes.com/2008/nov/25/local/me-thanksgiving25

40. World Net Daily, October 27, 2007 "Feather protest defies NCAA"
   http://www.wnd.com/news/article.asp?ARTICLE_ID=58377

   World Net Daily, October 27, 2006 "Are feathers 'hostile and abusive' to Indians?"
   http://www.wnd.com/news/article.asp?ARTICLE_ID=52648

41. World Net Daily, April, 16, 2008 "Bow your head, break the law!"
   http://www.wnd.com/index.php?fa=PAGE.view&pageId=61806

   World Net Daily, October 27, 2008 "Coach asks permission to bow head while players pray"
   http://www.wnd.com/index.php?fa=PAGE.view&pageId=79284

42. Rutherford.org Brief of *Amicus Curiae*—American Football Coaches Association in support of Marcus A. Borden.
   http://www.rutherford.org/pdf/coachesamicus.pdf

43. C-SPAN Video Library, January 7, 2009 "Economic Recovery Plan"
   http://www.c-spanvideo.org/program/283157-1&start=1563

44. Robert Reich's Blog, January 8, 2009 "The Stimulus: How to Create Jobs Without Them All Going to Skilled Professionals and White Male Construction Workers"
   http://robertreich.blogspot.com/2009/01/stimulus-how-to-create-jobs-without.html

45. C-SPAN Video Library, January 7, 2009 "Economic Recovery Plan"
   http://www.c-spanvideo.org/program/283157-1&start=1563

46. C-SPAN Video Library, January 7, 2009 "Economic Recovery Plan"
    http://www.c-spanvideo.org/program/283157-1&start=1563

47. The Washington Post, July 8, 2007 "Arizona's Border Burden" David
    S. Broder
    http://www.washingtonpost.com/wp-dyn/content/article/2007/07/06/
    AR2007070601929.html

48. Michelle Malkin, February 8, 2009 "Reid blocks bipartisan amendment
    requiring citizenship verification for stimulus recipients" Michelle Malkin
    http://michellemalkin.com/2009/02/08/reid-blocks-bipartisan-
    amendment-requiring-citizenship-checks-for-stimulus-recipients/

49. YouTube Video "Obama: Illegals Won't Be Covered Under My Plan.
    So, We'll Just Legalize The 12 Million Undocumented."
    http://www.youtube.com/watch?v=91Tl671xASM&feature=play
    er_embedded

50. The New York Times, February 26, 2009 "Secretary Seeks Review of
    Immigration Raid"
    http://www.nytimes.com/2009/02/26/washington/26immig.html

51. CNN.com Transcript of an interview with Janet Napolitano, April 19,
    2009 on "State of the Union With John King"
    http://transcripts.cnn.com/TRANSCRIPTS/0904/19/sotu.01.html

52. The New York Times, August 11, 2009 "Napolitano Focuses on
    Immigration Enforcement" James C. McKinley Jr.
    http://www.nytimes.com/2009/08/12/us/12border.html?_r=1&fta=y

53. Fox News, March 18, 2009 "Pelosi Tells Illegal Immigrants That Work
    Site Raids are Un-American" William Lajeunesse
    http://www.foxnews.com/politics/2009/03/18/pelosi-tells-illegal-
    immigrants-work-site-raids-american/

54. Hot Air website, July 14, 2008 "Obama: Immigration enforcement =
    terror" Ed Morrissey
    http://hotair.com/archives/2008/07/14/obama-immigration-enforce-
    ment-terror/

55. The New York Times, November 17, 2007 "Immigration Quandary: A Mother Torn From Her Baby" Julia Preston
http://www.nytimes.com/2007/11/17/us/17citizen.html

56. Rhetoric Wars website, November 12, 2008 "Conjunction Disjunction"
http://www.rhetoricwars.com/

57. Glenn Beck website, August 26, 2009 "Maher: America, you're stupid"
http://www.glennbeck.com/content/articles/article/198/29737/

58. YouTube Video "Bill Maher offering his opinion" Video of a July 27, 2009 interview on CNN.com
http://www.youtube.com/watch?v=rWWHHNeGMss

59. Business & Media Institute, August 25, 2009 "HBO's Maher: Americans too 'Stupid" so President Should Force ObamaCare into Law" Jeff Poor
http://businessandmedia.org/articles/2009/20090825120853.aspx

60. Freedom Eden website, August 25, 2009 "Bill Maher and Conan O'Brien, August 24"
http://freedomeden.blogspot.com/2009/08/bill-maher-and-conan-obrien-august-24.html

61. Glenn Beck website, August 26, 2009 "Maher: America, you're stupid"
http://www.glennbeck.com/content/articles/article/198/29737/

62. NewsBusters, April 16, 2009 "Garofalo: Tea Party Goers Are Racists Who Hate Black" Noel Sheppard
http://newsbusters.org/blogs/noel-sheppard/2009/04/16/garofalo-tea-partiers-are-all-racists-who-hate-black-president

63. Center for Immigration Studies, December 6, 2005 "The Impact of Non-Citizens on Congressional Apportionment" Steven A, Camarota, Director of Research, Center for Immigration Studies
http://www.cis.org/articles/2005/sactestimony120605.html

64. U.S. History website, "Washington's Farewell Address - 1796"
http://www.ushistory.org/documents/farewelladdress.htm

Early America website, "Georg Washington's Farewell Address To the People of the United States"
http://www.earlyamerica.com/earlyamerica/milestones/farewell/text.html

65. Arizona SB1070h from the official Arizona website.
http://www.azleg.gov/legtext/49leg/2r/bills/sb1070h.pdf

66. Arizona HB 2162c from the official Arizona website.
http://www.azleg.gov/legtext/49leg/2r/bills/hb2162c.pdf

67. YouTube website "Demi Moore and Ashton Kutcher's I Pledge Video"
Posted January 19, 2009
http://www.youtube.com/watch?v=51kAw4OTlA0

68. YouTube website, "Obama: My Plan Makes Electricity Rates Skyrocket"
Posted March 18, 2009
http://www.youtube.com/watch?v=HlTxGHn4sH4

San Francisco Chronicle, January 20, 2008 "Obama's straight-ahead style" John Diaz
http://www.sfgate.com/cgi-bin/article.cgi?f=/c/a/2008/01/20/EDIAUHASH.DTL

www.ingramcontent.com/pod-product-compliance
Lightning Source LLC
Chambersburg PA
CBHW030315290526
45785CB00001B/376